Billy Topsail, M. D.; a tale of adventure with Doctor Luke of the Labrador

Norman Duncan

BILLY TOPSAIL, M.D.

"BACK, YOU, CRACKER! BACK, YOU, SMOKE!"

(See page 85)

BILLY TOPSAIL, M.D.

A Tale of Adventure With Doctor Luke of the Labrador

By
NORMAN DUNCAN

ILLUSTRATED

New York Chicago Toronto.
Fleming H. Revell Company
London and Edinburgh

New York: 158 Fifth Avenue
Chicago: 17 North Wabash Ave.
Toronto: 25 Richmond Street, W.
London: 21 Paternoster Square
Edinburgh: 100 Princes Street

To the Reader

IN this tale of the seas and ice-floes of Newfoundland and Labrador, Billy Topsail adventures with Doctor Luke of the Labrador. There are thrilling passages in the book. The author is frank to admit the hair-raising quality of them. Indeed, they have tickled his own scalp. Well, it is proper that the hair of the reader should sometimes stand on end and his eyes pop wide. The author would be a poor teller of tales if he could not manage as much—a charlatan if he did not. Yet these thrilling passages are not the work of a saucy imagination, delighting in shudders, no matter what, but are all decently founded upon fact, true to the experience of the coast, as many a Newfoundlander, boy and man, could tell you.

Doctor Luke has often been mistaken for Doctor Wilfred Grenfell of the Deep Sea Mission. That should not be. No incident in this book is a transcript from Doctor Grenfell's long and heroic service. What Billy Topsail and Doctor

Luke encounter, however, is precisely what the Deep Sea Mission workers must encounter. It should be said, too, that as the tale is told of the spring of the year, when the ice breaks up and the floes come drifting out of the north with great storms, Newfoundland presents herself in her worst mood. Yet the sun shines in Newfoundland, tender enough in summer weather—there are flowers on the hills and warm winds on the sea; and such as learn to know the land come quickly to love her for her beauty and for her friendliness.

N. D.

New York, March, 1916.

CONTENTS

To
Elspeth's
Canadian Cousins
Russ and Dode, Tom and Kenn,
Rich and Logan, Mort and
Fos, Georgie,
and
all the girls of the con-
nection who will deign
to read the tale, Mar
and Buff, Frankie,
Bettie and Jean
when the time
comes,
with a wink and a challenge
to
Kathie Sweet.

BILLY TOPSAIL, M.D.

CHAPTER I

In Which It Is Hinted that Teddy Brisk Would Make a Nice Little Morsel o' Dog Meat, and Billy Topsail Begins an Adventure that Eventually Causes His Hair to Stand on End and Is Likely to Make the Reader's Do the Same

ONE dark night in the fall of the year, the trading-schooner *Black Bat*, of Ruddy Cove, slipped ashore on the rocks of Tight Cove, of the Labrador. She was frozen fast before she could be floated. And that was the end of her flitting about. It was the end, too, of Billy Topsail's rosy expectation of an hilarious return to his home at Ruddy Cove. Winter fell down next day. A great wind blew with snow and frost; and when the gale was blown out—the sun out and the sky blue again—it was out of the question to rip the *Black Bat* out of her icy berth in Tight Cove Harbour and put her on the tumbled way to Ruddy.

And that is how it came about that Billy Topsail passed the winter at Tight Cove, with Teddy Brisk, and in the spring of the year, when the ice was breaking up, fell in with Doctor Luke of the Labrador in a way that did not lack the aspects of an adventure of heroic proportions. It was no great hardship to pass the winter at Tight Cove: there was something to do all the while—trapping in the back country; and there was no uneasiness at home in Ruddy Cove—a wireless message from the station at Red Rock had informed Ruddy Cove of the fate of the *Black Bat* and the health and comfort of her crew.

And now for the astonishing tale of how Doctor Luke and Billy Topsail fell in together——

When Doctor Luke made Tight Cove, of the Labrador, in the course of his return to his little hospital at Our Harbour, it was dusk. His dogs were famished; he was himself worn lean with near five hundred miles of winter travel, which measured his northern round, and his komatik (sled) was occupied by an old dame of Run-by-Guess Harbour and a young man of Anxious Bight. The destitute old dame of Run-by-

Guess Harbour was to die of her malady in a cleanly peace; the young man of Anxious Bight was to be relieved of those remnants of a shoulder and good right arm that an accidental gunshot wound had left to endanger his life.

It was not fit weather for any man to be abroad—a biting wind, a frost as cold as death, and a black threat of snow; but Doctor Luke, on this desperate business of healing, was in haste, and the patients on the komatik were in need too urgent for any dawdling for rest by the way. Schooner Bay ice was to cross; he would put up for the night—that was all; he must be off at dawn, said he in his quick, high way.

From this news little Teddy Brisk's mother returned to the lamp-lit cottage by Jack-in-the-Box. It was with Teddy Brisk's mother that Billy Topsail was housed for the winter.

"Is I t' go, mum?" said Teddy.

Teddy Brisk's mother trimmed the lamp.

"He've a ol' woman, dear," she replied, "from Run-by-Guess."

Teddy Brisk's inference was decided.

"Then he've room for *me*," he declared; "an' I'm not sorry t' learn it."

"Ah, well, dear, he've also a poor young feller from Anxious Bight."

Teddy Brisk nodded.

"That's all about *that*," said he positively. "He've *no* room for me!"

Obviously there was no room for little Teddy Brisk on Doctor Luke's komatik. Little Teddy Brisk, small as he was, and however ingenious an arrangement might be devised, and whatever degree of compression might be attempted, and no matter what generous measure of patience might be exercised by everybody concerned, including the dogs—little Teddy Brisk of Tight Cove could not be stowed away with the old dame from Run-by-Guess Harbour and the young man of Anxious Bight.

There were twenty miles of bay ice ahead; the dogs were footsore and lean; the komatik was overflowing—it was out of the question. Nor could Teddy Brisk, going afoot, keep pace with the Doctor's hearty strides and the speed of the Doctor's team—not though he had the soundest little legs on the Labrador, and the longest on the Labrador, of his years, and the sturdiest, anywhere, of his growth.

As a matter of fact, one of Teddy Brisk's

legs was as stout and willing as any ten-year-old leg ever you saw; but the other had gone bad—not so recently, however, that the keen Doctor Luke was deceived in respect to the trouble, or so long ago that he was helpless to correct it.

Late that night, in the lamp-lit cottage by Jack-in-the-Box, the Doctor looked over the bad leg with a severely critical eye; and he popped more questions at Teddy Brisk, as Teddy Brisk maintained, than had ever before been exploded on anybody in the same length of time.

"Huh!" said he at last. "I can fix it."

"You can patch un up, sir?" cried Skipper Tom.

This was Thomas Brisk. The father of Teddy Brisk had been cast away, with the *Brotherly Love*, on the reef by Fly Away Head, in the Year of the Big Shore Catch. This old Thomas was his grandfather.

"No, no, no!" the Doctor complained. "I tell you I can *fix* it!"

"Will he be as good as new, sir?" said Teddy.

"Will he?" the Doctor replied. "Aha!" he laughed. "You leave that to the carpenter."

"As good as Billy Topsail's off shank?"

"I'll scrape that bad bone in there," said the Doctor, rubbing his hands in a flush of professional expectation; "and if it isn't as good as new when the job's finished I'll—I'll—why, I'll blush, my son: I'll blush all red and crimson and scarlet."

Teddy Brisk's mother was uneasy.

"Will you be usin' the knife, sir?"

"The knife? Certainly!"

"I'm not knowin'," said the mother, "what little Teddy will say t' that."

"What say, son?" the Doctor inquired

"Will it be you that's t' use the knife?" asked Teddy.

"Mm-m!" said the Doctor. He grinned and twinkled. "I'm the butcher, sir."

Teddy Brisk laughed. "That suits *me!*" said he.

"That's hearty!" the Doctor exclaimed. He was delighted. The trust was recompense. God knows it was welcome! "I'll fix you, Teddy boy," said he, rising. And to Skipper Thomas: "Send the lad over to the hospital as soon as you can, Skipper Thomas. When the ice goes out we'll be crowded to the roof at Our Harbour. It's the same way every spring.

Egad! they'll sweep in like the flakes of the first fall of snow! Now's the time. Make haste! We must have this done while I've a cot to spare."

"I will, sir."

"We're due for a break-up soon, I suppose—any day now; but this wind and frost will hold the ice in the bay for a while. You can slip the lad across any day. It must be pretty fair going out there. You can't bring him yourself, Skipper Thomas. Who can? Somebody here? Timothy Light? Old Sam's brother, isn't he? I know him. It's all arranged, then. I'll be looking for the lad in a day or two. You've plenty of dogs in Tight Cove, haven't you?"

"Oh, aye, sir," Skipper Thomas replied; 'we've *dogs*, sir—never you mind about that!"

"Whose dogs?"

"Timothy Light's dogs."

The Doctor grinned again.

"That pack!" said he.

"A saucy pack o' dogs!" said Teddy's mother. "It's mostly new this season. I don't like un! I'm fair afraid o' them, sir. That big Cracker, sir, that Timothy haves for bully an' leader—he've fair spoiled Timothy Light's whole team.

I'm none too fond o' that great dog, sir; an' I'll have my say about it."

Skipper Thomas laughed—as a man will at a woman's fears.

"No sheep's manners t' that pack," he drawled. "The team's all dawg."

"What isn't wolf!" the woman retorted.

"She've been afraid o' that Cracker," Skipper Thomas explained, "ever since he fetched a brace o' wolves out o' the timber. 'Twas as queer a sight, now, as ever you seed, sir. They hung round the harbour for a day an' a night. You might think, sir, that Cracker was showin' off his new quarters t' some friends from the back country. They two wolves seemed t' have knowed Cracker all their lives. I 'low that they *had* knowed ——"

"He's half wolf hisself."

"I 'low he's *all* wolf," Skipper Thomas admitted. This was not true. Cracker was not all wolf. "I never heard o' nobody that knowed where Cracker was born. That dog come in from the timber."

"A wicked crew—the pack o' them!"

"We've had a lean winter at Tight Cove, sir," said Skipper Thomas. "The dogs have gone marvellous hungry this past month, sir. They're just a wee bit savage."

"Spare your dog meat if you lack it," the Doctor advised. "I'll feed that team at Our Harbour."

Teddy Brisk put in:

"Timothy Light haves command o' that pack."

"I'm not so sure that he've command," Teddy Brisk's mother protested. "I'm not so sure that any man could command a shockin' pack like that. In case o' accident, now ——"

Skipper Thomas chucked his ample, glowing daughter-in-law under the chin.

"You loves that lad o' yourn!" he bantered.

"I does!"

"You're thinkin' he'd make a nice little morsel o' dog meat?"

"As for me," she laughed, "*I* could eat him!"

She caught little Teddy Brisk in her arms and kissed him all over his eager little face. And then Doctor Luke, with a laugh and a boyish "So long, Teddy Brisk! See you soon, old soldier!" vanished to his lodgings for the night.

CHAPTER II

In Which Timothy Light's Team of Ten Potential Outlaws is Considered, and There is a Significant Description of the Career of a Blood-Guilty, Ruined Young Dog, Which is in the Way of Making Desperate Trouble for Somebody

OF all this Billy Topsail had been an observer. To a good deal of it he had listened with an awakened astonishment. It did not appear to him that he would be concerned in what might grow out of the incident. He did not for a moment imagine, for example, that he would find himself in a situation wherein his hair would stand on end—that he would stand stripped naked in the north wind, confronting Death in a most unpleasant form. Nor was it that Doctor Luke's personality had stirred him to admiration—though that was true: for Doctor Luke had a hearty, cheery twinkling way with him, occasionally mixed with a proper austerity, that would have won any boy's admiration; but what particularly engaged Billy Topsail was something else—it was Doctor

Luke's confident assertion that he could cure little Teddy Brisk.

Billy Topsail knew something of doctors, to be sure; but he had never before quite realized their power; and that a man, being only human, after all, could take a knife in his hand, which was only a man's hand, after all, and so employ the knife that the painful, hampering leg of Teddy Brisk, which had placed a dreadful limitation on the little boy, would be made whole and useful again, caused Billy Topsail a good deal of deep reflection. If Doctor Luke could do that, why could not Billy Topsail learn to do it? It seemed to Billy Topsail to be a more admirable thing to be able to do than to sail a hundred-tonner in a gale of wind.

"Who *is* that man?" he asked.

"That's Doctor Luke," said Teddy's mother. "You know that."

"Well, who's Doctor Luke?"

"I don't know. He's jus' Doctor Luke. He've a wee hospital at Our Harbour. An' he heals folk. You'll find un go anywhere he's asked t' go if there's a poor soul in need. An' that's all *I* know about un."

"What does he do it for?"

"I reckon he wants to. An' anyhow, I'm glad he does do it. An' I reckon you'd be glad, too, if you had a little boy like Teddy."

"I *am* glad!" said Billy. "I think 'tis the most wonderful thing ever I heard of. An' I wish ——"

And the course of Billy Topsail's life moved inevitably on towards a nearing fate that he would have shuddered to contemplate had he foreseen it.

Well, now, there was but one team of dogs in Tight Cove. It was a happy circumstance. No dogs could have existed as a separate pack in the neighbourhood of Timothy Light's mob of potential outlaws. It was all very well for Timothy Light to pleasure his hobby and pride in the unsavoury collection. Timothy Light had command of his own team. It was quite another matter for the timid mothers of Tight Cove. Timothy Light's dogs had a bad name. As neighbours they deserved it, whatever their quality on the trail—a thieving, snarling crew.

To catch Timothy Light in the act of feeding his team was enough to establish an antipathy in the beholder—to see the old man beat off the rush of the pack with a biting walrus whip while he spread the bucket of frozen fish; to watch him, then, leap away from the ferocious onset; and to be witness of the ravenous anarchy of the scramble—a free fight, dwindling, at last, to melancholy yelps and subsiding in the licking of the small wounds of the encounter. Timothy Light was a fancier of dog flesh, as a man may be devoted to horse-flesh; and the object of his selective taste was what he called go-an'-gumption.

"The nearer the wolf," said he, "the better the dog."

It was to accord with this theory—which is a fallacy as a generalization—that he had evolved the team of ten that he had.

"I'm free t' say," he admitted, "that this here Cracker o' mine is none too tame. He've the wolf in him—that's so. As a wolf, with the pack in the timber, he'd be a bad wolf; as a dog in harbour he's a marvellous wicked rogue. He've a eye as bitter as frost. Did you mark it? He leaves it fool all over a person in a laughin' sort o' fashion an' never stop on the spot he really wants t' look at—except jus' once in a while. An' then it darts t' the throat an' away again; an' Cracker thinks, jus' as plain as speech:

"'Oh, Lord, wouldn't I like t' fix my teeth in there!'

"Still an' all," the old man concluded, "he yields t' command. A tap on the snout goes a long way with Cracker. He've a deal o' wolf's blood—that one has; but he's as big a coward, too, as a wolf, an' there's no danger in him when he's overmastered. Still an' all"—with a shrug—"I'd not care t' lose my whip an' stumble an' fall on the trail in the dusk when he haven't been fed for a while."

Cracker had come to Tight Cove in a dog trade of questionable propriety. Cracker had not at once taken to the customs and dogs of Tight Cove; he had stood off, sullen, alert, still—head low, king-hairs lifted, eyes flaring. It was an attitude of distrust, dashed with melancholy, rather than of challenge. Curiosity alone maintained it through the interval required for decision. Cracker was deliberating.

There was Tight Cove and a condition of servitude to Timothy Light; there were the free, wild, famishing spaces of the timber beyond. Cracker must choose between them.

All at once, then, having brooded himself to a

conclusion, Cracker began to wag and laugh in a fashion the most ingratiating to be imagined: and thereupon he fought himself to an established leadership of Timothy Light's pack, as though to dispose, without delay, of that necessary little preliminary to distinction. And subsequently he accepted the mastery of Timothy Light and fawned his way into security from the alarmed abuse of the harbour folk; and eventually he settled himself comfortably into the routine of Tight Cove life.

There were absences. These were invariably foreshadowed, at first, by yawning and a wretched depth of boredom. Cracker was ashamed of his intentions. He would even attempt to conceal his increasing distaste for the commonplaces of an existence in town by a suspiciously subservient obedience to all the commands of Timothy Light. It was apparent that he was preparing for an excursion to the timber; and after a day or two of whimpering restlessness he would vanish.

It was understood, then, that Cracker was off a-visiting of his cronies. Sometimes these absences would be prolonged. Cracker had been gone a month—had been caught, once, in a distant glance, with a pack of timber wolves, from whom he had fled to hiding, like a boy detected in bad company. Cracker had never failed, however, to return from his abandoned course, in reasonable season, as lean and ragged as a prodigal son, and in a chastened mood, to the respectability and plenty of civilization, even though it implied an acquiescence in the exigency of hard labour.

Timothy Light excused the dog.

"He've got t' have his run abroad," said he. "I 'low that blood is thicker than water."

Cracker had a past. Timothy Light knew something of Cracker's past. What was respectable he had been told, with a good deal of elaboration—concerning Cracker's feats of endurance on the long trail, for example, accomplished with broken shoes, or no shoes at all, and bloody, frosted feet; and relating, with warm, wide-eyed detail of a persuasively conscientious description, to Cracker's cheerful resistance of the incredible pangs of hunger on a certain celebrated occasion.

Moreover, Cracker was a bully of parts. Cracker could bully a discouraged team into a forlorn endeavour of an amazing degree of power and courage. "As clever a dog as ever you seed, sir! No shirkin'—ecod!—with Cracker t' keep watch on the dogs an' snap at the heels an' haunches o' the loafers." It was all true: Cracker was a powerful, clever, masterful, enduring beast in or out of harness, and a merciless driver of the dogs he led and had mastered.

"Give the devil his due!" Timothy Light insisted.

What was disreputable in Cracker's past—in the course of the dog trade of questionable propriety referred to—Timothy Light had been left to exercise his wit in finding out for himself. Cracker was from the north—from Jolly Cove, by the Hen-an'-Chickens. And what Timothy Light did not know was this: Cracker had there been concerned in an affair so doubtful, and of a significance so shocking, that, had the news of it got abroad in Tight Cove, the folk would have taken the customary precaution as a defensive measure, in behalf of the children on the roads after dark, and as a public warning to all the dogs of Tight Cove, of hanging Cracker by the neck until he was dead.

Long John Wall, of Jolly Cove, on the way to the Post at Little Inlet, by dog team, in January weather, had been caught by the snow between Grief Head and the Tall Old Man; and Long John Wall had perished on the ice—they found his komatik and clean bones in the spring of the year; but when the gale blew out, Long John Wall's dogs had returned to Jolly Cove in a fawning humour and a suspiciously well-fed condition.

The Jolly Cove youngster, the other party to the dog trade, neglected to inform Timothy Light—whose eyes had fallen enviously on the smoky, taut, splendid brute—that this selfsame Cracker which he coveted had bullied and led Long John Wall's team on that tragic and indubitably bloody occasion.

His philosophy was ample to his need.

"In a dog trade," thought he with his teeth bare, when the bargain was struck, "'tis every man for hisself."

And so this blood-guilty, ruined young dog had come unsuspected to Tight Cove.

CHAPTER III

In Which Timothy Light's Famished Dogs Are Committed to the Hands of Billy Topsail and a Tap on the Snout is Recommended in the Probable Case of Danger

IT is no great trick to make Tight Cove of the Labrador from the sea. There is no chart, of course. Nor is any chart of the little harbours needed for safe sailing, as long as the songs of the coast are preserved in the heads of the skippers that sail it. And so you may lay with confidence a bit west of north from the Cape Norman light—and raise and round the Scotchman's Breakfast of Ginger Head: whereupon a straightaway across Schooner Bay to the Thimble, and, upon nearer approach to the harbour water of the Cove —

> When Bill Pott's P'int you is abreast,
> Dane's Rock bears due west;
> An' west-nor'west you must steer,
> 'Til Brimstone Head do appear.
>
> The tickle's narrow, not very wide;
> The deepest water's on the starboard side;
> When in the harbour you is shot,
> Four fathoms you has got —

and there you are: harboured within stone's throw of thirty hospitable cottages, with their stages and flakes clustered about, like offspring, and all clinging to the cliffs with the grip of a colony of mussels. They encircle the quiet, deep water of the Cove, lying in a hollow of Bill Pott's Point, Dane's Rock, and the little head called Brimstone.

Winter was near done, at Tight Cove, when Doctor Luke made the lights of the place from the north. Presently the sun and southwesterly winds of spring would spread the coast with all the balmy, sudden omens of summer weather, precisely as the first blast from the north, in a single night of the fall of the year, had blanketed the land with snow, and tucked it in, with enduring frost, for the winter to come. With these warm winds, the ice in Schooner Bay would move to sea, with the speed of a thief in flight. It would break up and vanish in a night, with all that was on it (including the folk who chanced to be caught on it)—a great, noisy commotion, and swift clearing out, this removal to the open.

And the ice would drift in, again, with contrary winds, and choke the bay, accompanied by Arctic ice from the current beyond, and depart and come once more, and take leave, in a season of its own willful choosing, for good and all When Doctor Luke made off across the bay, leaving Teddy Brisk to follow, by means of Timothy Light's komatik and scrawny dogs, Schooner Bay had already gone rotten, in a spell of southerly weather. The final break-up was restrained only by an interval of unseasonable frost.

A favourable wind would tear the field loose from the cliffs and urge it to sea.

Teddy Brisk could not go at once to Doctor Luke's hospital at Our Harbour. There came a mild spell—the wind went to the south and west in the night; a splashing fall of tepid southern rain swept the dry white coats in gusts and a melting drizzle; and, following on these untimely showers, a day or two of sunshine and soft breezes set the roofs smoking, the icicles dissolving, the eaves running little streams of water, the cliffs dripping a promise of shy spring flowers, and packed the snow and turned the harbour roads to slush, and gathered pools and shallow lakes of water on the rotting ice of the bay.

Schooner Bay was impassable; the trail was

deep and sticky and treacherous—a broken, rotten, imminently vanishing course. And seaward, in the lift of the waves, vast fragments of the field were shaking themselves free and floating off; and the whole wide body of ice, from Rattle Brook, at the bottom of the bay, to the great heads of Thimble and the Scotchman's Breakfast, was striving to break away to the open under the urge of the wind.

Teddy Brisk's adventure to Our Harbour must wait for frost and still weather; and wait it did —until in a shift of the weather there came a day when all that was water was frozen stiff overnight, and the wind fell away to a doubtful calm, and the cliffs of Ginger Head were a loom in the frosty distance across the bay.

"Pack that lad, mum," said Skipper Thomas then. "'Tis now or never."

"I don't like the look of it," the mother complained.

"I warns you, mum—you're too fond o' that lad."

"I'm anxious. The bay's rotten. You knows that, sir—a man as old as you. Another southerly wind would shatter ——"

"Ecod! You'll coddle that wee lad t' death."

Teddy Brisk's mother laughed.

"Not me!" said she.

A cunning idea occurred to Skipper Thomas.

"Or cowardice!" he grumbled.

Teddy Brisk's mother started. She stared in doubt at old Skipper Thomas. Her face clouded. She was grim.

"I'd do nothin' so wicked as that, sir," said she. "I'll pack un up."

It chanced that Timothy Light was sunk in a melancholy regard of his physical health when Skipper Thomas went to arrange for the dogs. He was discovered hugging a red-hot bogie in his bachelor cottage of turf and rough-hewn timber by the turn to Sunday-School Hill. And a woebegone old fellow he was: a sight to stir pity and laughter—with his bottles and plasters, his patent-medicine pamphlets, his drawn, gloomy countenance, and his determination to "draw off" the indisposition by way of his lower extremities with a plaster of renowned power.

"Nothin' stronger, Skipper Thomas, knowed t' the science o' medicine an' the"—Skipper Timothy did not hesitate over the obstacle—"the prac-t'-tie-on-ers thereof," he groaned; "an' she've begun t' pull too. Ecod! but she's drawin'! Mm-m-m! There's power for you! An' if she don't pull the pain out o' the toes o' my two feet"—Skipper Timothy's feet were swathed in plaster; his pain was elsewhere; the course of its exit was long—"I'm free t' say that nothin' will budge my complaint. Mm-m! Ecod! b'y, but she've sure begun t' draw!"

Skipper Timothy bade Skipper Thomas sit himself down, an' brew himself a cup o' tea, an' make himself t' home, an' feel free o' the place, the while he should entertain and profit himself with observing the operation of the plaster of infallible efficacy in the extraction of pain.

"What's gone wrong along o' you?" Skipper Thomas inquired.

"I been singin' pretty hearty o' late," Skipper Timothy moaned—he was of a musical turn and given frequently to a vigorous recital of the Psalms and Paraphrases—"an' I 'low I've strained my stummick."

Possibly Skipper Timothy could not distinguish, with any degree of scientific accuracy, between the region of his stomach and the region of his lungs—a lay confusion, perhaps, in the matter of terms and definite boundaries ; he had been known to mistake his liver for his heart in the indulgence of a habit of pessimistic diagnosis. And whether he was right in this instance or not, and whatever the strain involved in his vocal effort, which must have tried all the muscles concerned, he was now coughing himself purple in the face—a symptom that held its mortal implication of the approach of what is called the lung trouble and the decline.

The old man was not fit for the trail—no cruise to Our Harbour for him next day; he was on the stocks and out of commission. Ah, well, then, would he trust his dogs? Oh, aye; he would trust his team free an' willin'. An' might Billy Topsail drive the team? Oh, aye; young Billy Topsail might drive the team an he had the spirit for the adventure. Let Billy Topsail keep un down—*keep the brutes down*, ecod!—and no trouble would come of it.

"A tap on the snout t' mend their manners," Skipper Timothy advised. "A child can overcome an' manage a team like that team o' ten."

And so it was arranged that Billy Topsail should drive Teddy Brisk to Our Harbour next day.

CHAPTER IV

In Which the Komatik is Foundered, the Dogs Draw Their Own Conclusions from the Misfortune and Prepare to Take Advantage, Cracker Attempts a Theft and Gets a Clip on the Snout, and Billy Topsail and Teddy Brisk Confront a Situation of Peril with Composure, Not Knowing the Ultimate Disaster that Impends

BILLY TOPSAIL was now sixteen years old—near seventeen, to be exact; and he was a lusty, well-grown lad, who might easily have been mistaken for a man, not only because of his inches, but because of an assured, competent glance of the eye. Born at Ruddy Cove of Newfoundland, and the son of a fisherman, he was a capable chap in his native environment. And what natural aptitude he possessed for looking after himself in emergencies had been developed and made more courageous and acute by the adventurous life he had lived—as anybody may know, indeed, who cares to peruse the records of those incidents as elsewhere set down. As assistant to the clerk of the trader *Black Bat*, he had served well; and it is probable that he would some day have been a clerk himself, and eventually a trader, had not the adventure upon which he was embarking with Teddy Brisk interrupted his career by opening a new vista for his ambition.

Billy Topsail and Teddy Brisk set out in blithe spirits for Doctor Luke's hospital at Our Harbour. A dawn of obscure and disquieting significance; a hint of milder weather in the growing day; a drear, gray sky thickening to drab and black, past noon; a puff of southerly wind and a slosh of rain; a brisk gale, lightly touched with frost, running westerly, with snow, in a close, encompassing cloud of great wet flakes; lost landmarks; dusk falling, and a black night imminent, with high wind—and Billy Topsail's team of ten went scrambling over an unexpected ridge and foundered the komatik.

It was a halt—no grave damage done; it was nothing to worry a man—not then.

Young Billy Topsail laughed; and little Teddy Brisk chuckled from the tumbled depths of his dogskin robes; and the dogs, on their haunches now, a panting, restless half-circle—the Labrador dogs run in individual traces—viewed the spill with shamefaced amusement. Yet Billy Topsail was confused and lost. Snow and dusk were impenetrable; the barricades and cliffs of Ginger Head, to which he was bound, lay somewhere in the snow beyond—a mere general direction. It is nothing, however, to be lost. Daylight and clearing weather infallibly disclose the lay of the land.

A general direction is good enough; a man proceeds confidently on the meager advantage.

It was interesting for the dogs—this rowdy pack from Tight Cove. They were presently curious. It was a break in the routine of the road. The thing concerned them nearly. What the mischief was the matter? Something was up! Here was no mere pause for rest. The man was making no arrangements to move along. And what now? Amusement gave place to an alert observation of the course of the unusual incident.

The dogs came a little closer. It was not an attitude of menace. They followed Billy Topsail's least movement with jerks of concern and starts of surprise; and they reflected—inquiring amazed. Day's work done? Camp for the night? Food? What next, anyhow? It was snowing. Thick weather, this! Thick's bags—this palpable dusk! No man could see his way in a gale like this. A man had his limitations and customs. This man would camp. There would be food in reward of the day's work. Was there never to be any food? There must be food! Now—at last! Oh, sure—why, sure—sure—sure there'd be something to eat when the man went into camp!

Mm-m? No? Was the new man going to starve 'em all to death!

Big Cracker, of this profane, rowdy crew, sidled to the sled. This was in small advances—a sly encroachment at a time. His object was plain to the pack. It was theft. They watched him in a trance of expectant interest. What would happen to Cracker? Wait and see! Follow Cracker? Oh, wait and see, first, what happened to Cracker. And Cracker sniffed at the tumbled robes. The pack lifted its noses and sniffed, too, and opened its eyes wide, and exchanged opinions, and kept watch, in swift, scared glances, on Billy Topsail; and came squirming nearer, as though with some intention altogether remote from the one precisely in mind.

From this intrusion—appearing to be merely an impudent investigation—Cracker was driven off with a quick, light clip of the butt of the walrus whip on the snout. "Keep the brutes down! Keep un down—ecod!—an' no trouble would come of it." And down went Cracker. He leaped away and bristled, and snarled, and crawled, whimpering then, to his distance; whereupon the pack took warning. Confound the man!—he was too quick with the whip. Cracker had intended no mischief, had he?

After that the big Cracker curled up and sulked himself to sleep.

"I 'low we're close t' Ginger Head," said Billy Topsail.

"Ah, no, b'y."

"I seed the nose o' the Scotchman's Breakfast a while back."

"We're t' the south o' that by three mile."

"We isn't."

"We is."

"Ah, well, anyhow we'll stop the night where we is. The snow blinds a man."

"That's grievous," Teddy Brisk complained.

"I wisht we was over the barricades an' safe ashore. The bay's all rotten. My mother says ——"

"You isn't timid, is you?"

"Me? No. My mother says ——"

"Ah, you is a bit timid, Teddy."

"Who? Me? I is not. But my mother says the wind would just ——"

"Just a wee bit timid!"

"Ah, well, Billy, I isn't never been out overnight afore. An' my mother says if the wind blows a gale from the west, south or sou'-west ——"

"Never you mind about that, Skipper Teddy. We've something better t' think about than the way the wind blows. The wind's full o' notions. I've no patience t' keep my humour waitin' on what she does. Now you listen t' me: I got bread, an' I got 'lasses, an' I got tea, an' I got a kettle. I got birch all split t' hand, t' save the weight of an axe on the komatik; an' I got birch rind, an' I got matches. 'Twill be a scoff"—feast—"Skipper Teddy. Mm-m! Ecod! My belly's in a clamour o' greed. The only thing I isn't got is dog meat. Save for that, Skipper Teddy, we're complete."

Teddy Brisk renewed his complaint.

"I wisht," said he, "the wind would switch t' sea. Once on a time my grand ——"

"Never you mind about that."

"Once on a time my grandfather was cotched by the snow in a gale o' wind off ——"

"Ah, you watch how clever I is at makin' a fire on the ice! Never you mind about the will o' the wind. 'Tis a foolish habit t' fall into."

Billy Topsail made the fire. The dogs squatted in the offing. Every eye was on the operation. It was interesting, of course. Nothing escaped notice. Attention was keen and inclusive. It would flare high—a thrill ran through the wide-mouthed, staring circle—and expire in disappointment. Interesting, to be sure: yet going into camp on the ice was nothing out of the way. The man would spend the night where he was—that was all. It portended no extraordinary departure from the customs—no opportunity. And the man was alert and capable. No; nothing stimulating in the situation—nothing to be taken advantage of.

Billy Topsail was laughing. Teddy Brisk chattered all the while. Neither was in difficulty. Nor was either afraid of anything. It was not an emergency. There was no release of authority. And when the circumstances of the affair, at last, had turned out to be usual in every respect, interest lapsed, as a matter of course; and the pack, having presently exhausted the distraction of backbiting, turned in to sleep, helped to this good conduct by a crack of the whip.

"Not another word out o' you!" Billy Topsail scolded. "You'll be fed full the morrow."

Almost at once it fell very dark. The frost increased; the snow turned to dry powder and the wind jumped to half a gale, veering to the sou'west. Teddy Brisk, with the bread and tea and molasses stowed away where bread and tea and molasses best serve such little lads as he, was propped against the komatik, wrapped up in his dogskin robes as snug as you like. The fire was roaring, and the circle of the night was safe and light and all revealed, in its flickering blaze and radiant, warm red glow.

Billy Topsail fed the fire hot; and Billy Topsail gave Teddy Brisk riddles to rede; and Billy Topsail piped Teddy Brisk a song or two—such a familiar song of the coast as this:

'Way down on Pigeon Pond Island,
When daddy comes home from swilein'
  Maggoty fish hung up in the air,
  Fried in maggoty butter;
Cakes an' tea for breakfast,
Pork an' duff for dinner,
Cakes an' tea for supper—
'Way down on Pigeon Pond Island,
When daddy comes home from swilein'.[1]

Whatever was bitter and inimical in the wind and dark and driving mist of snow was chased out of mind by the warm fire and companionable behaviour.

It was comfortable on the ice: it was a picnic —a bright adventure; and Teddy Brisk was as cozy and dry and content as ——

"I likes it, Billy," said he. "I jus' fair loves it here!"

"You does, b'y? I'm proud o' you!"

"'Way out here on the ice. Mm-m! Yes, sirree! I'm havin' a wonderful happy time, Billy."

"I'm glad o' that now!"

"An' I feels safe ——"

"Aye, b'y!'

"An' I'm's warm ——"

"Sure, you is!"

[1] Sealing.

"An' I'm's sleepy ——"

"You go t' sleep, lad."

"My mother says, if the wind ——"

"Never you mind about that. I'll take care o' you—never fear!"

"You would, in a tight place, wouldn't you, Billy, b'y?"

"Well, I 'low I would!"

"Yes, sirree! You'd take care o' me!"

"You go t' sleep, lad, an' show yourself an old hand at stoppin' out overnight."

"Aye, Billy; but my mother says ——"

"Never you mind about that."

"Ah, well, my mother ——"

And Teddy Brisk fell asleep.

CHAPTER V

In Which the Wind Goes to Work, the Ice Behaves in an Alarming Way, Billy Topsail Regrets, for Obvious Reasons, Having to Do with the Dogs, that He Had Not Brought an Axe, and Teddy Brisk Protests that His Mother Knew Precisely What She was Talking About

WELL, now, Teddy Brisk fell asleep, and presently, too, Billy Topsail, in his wolfskin bag, got the better of his anxious watch on the wind and toppled off. The dogs were already asleep, each covered with a slow-fashioning blanket of snow—ten round mounds, with neither snout nor hair to show. The fire failed: it was dark; and the wind blew up—and higher. A bleak place, this, on Schooner Bay, somewhere between the Thimble and the Scotchman's Breakfast of Ginger Head; yet there was no hardship in the night—no shivering, blue agony of cold, but full measure of healthful comfort. The dogs were warm in their coverings of snow and Billy Topsail was warm in his wolfskin bag; and Teddy Brisk, in his dogskin robes, was in a flush and soft sweat of sound sleep, as in his cot in the cottage by Jack-in-the-Box, at Tight Cove.

It was a gale of wind by this time. The wind came running down the bay from Rattle Brook; and it tore persistently at the ice, urging it out. It was a matter of twenty miles from the Thimble, across Schooner Bay, to the Scotchman's Breakfast of Ginger Head, and a matter of thirty miles inland to Rattle Brook—wherefrom you may compute the area of the triangle for yourself and bestir your own imagination, if you can, to apply the pressure of a forty-mile gale to the vast rough surface of the bay.

Past midnight the ice yielded to the irresistible urge of the wind.

Crack! The noise of the break zigzagged in the distance and approached, and shot past near by, and rumbled away like a crash of brittle thunder. Billy Topsail started awake. There was a crackling confusion—in the dark, all roundabout, near and far—like the crumpling of an infinitely gigantic sheet of crisp paper: and then nothing but the sweep and whimper of the wind—those familiar, unportentous sounds, in their mild monotony, like dead silence in contrast with the first splitting roar of the break-up.

Billy Topsail got out of his wolfskin bag. The dogs were up; they were terrified—growling and bristling; and they fawned close to Billy, as dogs will to a master in a crisis of ghostly fear. Billy drove them off; he whipped them into the dark. The ice had broken from the cliffs and was split in fields and fragments. It would move out and go abroad with the high southwest wind. That was bad enough, yet not, perhaps, a mortal predicament—the wind would not run out from the southwest forever; and an escape ashore from a stranded floe would be no new thing in the experience of the coast. To be marooned on a pan of ice, however, with ten famishing dogs of unsavoury reputation, and for God only knew how long—it taxed a man's courage to contemplate the inevitable adventure!

A man could not corner and kill a dog at a time; a man could not even catch a dog—not on a roomy pan of ice, with spaces for retreat. Nor could a man escape from a dog if he could not escape from the pan; nor could a man endure, in strength and wakefulness, as long as a dog. Billy Topsail saw himself attempt the death of one of the pack—the pursuit of Cracker, for example, with a club torn from the komatik. Cracker would easily keep his distance and paw the ice, head down, eyes alert and burning; and Cracker would withdraw and dart out of reach, and swerve away. And Smoke and Tucker and Scrap, and the rest of the pack, would all the while be creeping close behind, on the lookout for a fair opportunity.

No; a man could not corner and kill a dog at a time. A man could not beat a wolf in the open; and these dogs, which roamed the timber and sprang from it, would maneuver like wolves—a patient waiting for some lapse from caution or the ultimate moment of weakness; and then an overwhelming rush. Billy Topsail knew the dogs of his own coast. He knew his own dogs; all he did not know about his own dogs was that Cracker had been concerned in a dubious affair on the ice off the Tall Old Man. These dogs had gone on short rations for a month. When the worst came to the worst—the pan at sea—they would attack.

Teddy Brisk, too, was wide awake. A thin little plaint broke in on Billy Topsail's reflections.

"Is you there, Billy?"

"Aye, I'm here. You lie still, Teddy."

"What's the matter with the dogs, Billy?"

"They're jus' a bit restless. Never you mind about the dogs. I'll manage the dogs."

"You didn't fetch your axe, did you, Billy?"

"Well, no, Skipper Teddy—no; I didn't."

"That's what I thought. Is the ice broke loose?"

"Ah, now, Teddy, never you mind about the ice."

"Is she broke loose?"

"Ah, well—maybe she have broke loose."

"She'll move t' sea in this wind, won't she?"

"Never you mind ——"

"Won't she?"

"Ah, well, she may take a bit of a cruise t' sea."

Teddy Brisk said nothing to this. An interval of silence fell. And then Teddy plaintively again:

"My mother said ——"

Billy Topsail's rebuke was gentle:

"You isn't goin' t' cry for your mother, is you?"

"Oh, I isn't goin' t' cry for my mother!"

"Ah, no! You isn't. No growed man would."

"All I want t' say," said Teddy Brisk in a saucy flash of pride, "is that my mother was right!"

CHAPTER VI

In Which the Sudden Death of Cracker is Contemplated as a Thing to Be Desired, Billy Topsail's Whip Disappears, a Mutiny is Declared and the Dogs Howl in the Darkness

PAST twelve o'clock and the night as black as a wolf's throat, with the wind blowing a forty-mile gale, thick and stifling with snow, and the ice broken up in ragged pans of varying, secret area—it was no time for any man to stir abroad from the safe place he occupied. There were patches of open water forming near by, and lanes of open water widening and shifting with the drift and spreading of the ice; and somewhere between the cliffs and the moving pack, which had broken away from them, there was a long pitfall of water in the dark. The error of putting the dogs in the traces and attempting to win the shore in a forlorn dash did not even present itself to Billy Topsail's experienced wisdom. Billy Topsail would wait for dawn, to be sure of his path and direction; and meantime—there being no occasion for action—he got back into his wolfskin bag and settled himself for sleep.

It was not hard to go to sleep. Peril of this sort was familiar to Billy Topsail—precarious situations, with life at stake, created by wind, ice, reefs, fog and the sea. There on the ice the situation was completely disclosed and beyond control. Nothing was to be manipulated. Nothing threatened, at any rate, for the moment. Consequently Billy Topsail was not afraid. Had he discovered himself all at once alone in a city; had he been required to confront a garter snake—he had never clapped eyes on a snake——

Placidly reflecting on the factors of danger to be dealt with subsequently, Billy Topsail caught ear, he thought, of a sob and whimper from the midst of Teddy Brisk's dogskin robes. This was the little fellow's first full-fledged adventure. He had been in scrapes before—the little dangers of the harbour and the adjacent rocks and waters and wilderness; gusts of wind, the lop of the sea; the confusion of the near-by back country, and the like of that; but he had never been cast away like the grown men of Tight Cove. And these passages, heroic as they are, and stimulating as they may be to the ambition of the little fellows who listen o' winter nights, are drear and terrifying when first encountered.

Teddy Brisk was doubtless wanting his mother. Perhaps he sobbed. Yet he had concealed his fear and homesickness from Billy Topsail; and that was stoicism enough for any lad of his years—even a lad of the Labrador. Billy Topsail offered him no comfort. It would have shamed the boy to comfort him openly. Once ashore again Teddy Brisk would want to boast, like his elders, and to spin his yarn:

"Well now, lads, there we was, ecod! 'way out there on the ice, me 'n' Billy Topsail; an' the wind was blowin' a gale from the sou'west, an' the snow was flyin' as thick as ever you seed the snow fly, an' the ice was goin' out t' sea on the jump. An' I says t' Billy: 'I'm goin' t' sleep, Billy—an' be blowed t' what comes of it!' An' so I falled asleep as snug an' warm; an' then ——"

Billy Topsail ignored the sob and whimper from the depths of the dogskin robes.

"The lad haves t' be hardened," he reflected.

Dawn was windy. It was still snowing—a

frosty mist of snow. Billy Topsail put the dogs in the traces and stowed Teddy Brisk away in the komatik. The dogs were uneasy. Something out of the way? What the mischief was the matter? They came unwillingly. It seemed they must be sensing a predicament. Billy Topsail whipped them to their work and presently they bent well enough to the task.

Snow fell all that day. There were glimpses of Ginger Head. In a rift of the gale Teddy Brisk caught sight of the knob of the Scotchman's Breakfast.

Always, however, the way ashore was barred by open water. When Billy Topsail caught sight of the Scotchman's Breakfast for the last time it was in the southwest. This implied that the floe had got beyond the heads of the bay and was moving into the waste reaches of the open sea. At dusk Billy had circled the pan twice—hoping for chance contact with another pan, to the east, and another, and still another; and thus a path to shore. It was a big pan—a square mile or more as yet. When the pinch came, if the pinch should come, Billy thought, the dogs would not be hampered for room.

Why not kill the dogs? No; not yet. They

were another man's dogs. In the morning, if the wind held offshore ——

Wind and snow would fail. There would be no harsher weather. Billy Topsail made a little fire with his last billets of birchwood. He boiled the kettle and spread a thick slice of bread with a meager discoloration of molasses for Teddy Brisk. What chiefly interested Teddy Brisk was the attitude of the dogs. It was not obedient. There was swagger in it. A crack of the whip sent them leaping away, to be sure; but they intruded again at once—and mutinously persisted in the intrusion.

Teddy Brisk put out a diffident hand towards Smoke. Smoke was an obsequious brute. Ashore he would have been disgustingly grateful for the caress. Now he would not accept it at all. He snarled and sprang away. It was a defiant breach of discipline. What was the matter with the dogs? They had gone saucy all at once. The devil was in the dogs. Nor would they lie down; they withdrew, at last, in a pack, their hunger discouraged, and wandered restlessly in the failing light near by.

Teddy Brisk could not account for this singular behaviour.

It alarmed him.

"Ah, well," said Billy Topsail, "they're all savage with hunger."

"Could you manage with nine, Billy?"

Billy Topsail laughed.

"With ease, my son," said he, "an' glad of it!"

"Is you strong enough t' kill a dog?"

"I'll find that out, Teddy, when the time comes."

"I was 'lowin' that one dog would feed the others an' keep un mild till we gets ashore."

"I've that selfsame thing in mind."

Teddy said eagerly:

"Kill Cracker, Billy!"

"Cracker! Already? 'Twould be sheer murder."

"Aye, kill un now, Billy—ah, kill un right away now, won't you, b'y? That dog haves a grudge on me. He've been watchin' me all day long."

"Ah, no! Hush now, Teddy!"

"I knows that dog, Billy!"

"Ah, now! The wind'll change afore long. We'll drift ashore—maybe in the mornin' An' then ——"

"He've his eye on me, Billy!"

Billy Topsail rose.

"You see my whip anywhere?"

"She's lyin' for'ard o' the komatik."

"She's not."

"She was."

"She've gone, b'y!"

"Ecod! Billy, Cracker haves her!"

It was not yet dark. Cracker was sitting close. It was an attitude of jovial expectation. He was on his haunches—head on one side and tail flapping the snow; and he had the walrus whip in his mouth. Apparently he was in the mood to pursue a playful exploit. When Billy Topsail approached he retreated—a little; and when Billy Topsail rushed he dodged, with ease and increasing delight. When Billy Topsail whistled him up and patted to him, and called "Hyuh! Hyuh!" and flattered him with "Good ol' dog!" he yielded nothing more than a deepened attention to the mischievous pleasure in hand.

Always he was beyond reach—just beyond reach. It was tantalizing.

Billy Topsail lost his temper. This was a blunder. It encouraged the dog. To recover the whip was an imperative precaution; but Billy could not accomplish it in a temper Cracker was willful and agile and determined; and when he had tired—it seemed—of his taunting game, he whisked away, with the pack in chase, and was lost to sight in the gale. It fell dark then; and presently, far away a dog howled, and there was an answering howl, and a chorus of howls. They were gone for good. It was a mutiny. Billy knew that his authority had departed with the symbol of it.

He did not see the whip again.

CHAPTER VII

In Which a Blazing Club Plays a Salutary Part, Teddy Brisk Declares the Ways of His Mother, and Billy Topsail Looks Forward to a Battle that No Man Could Win

NEXT night—a starlit time then, and the wind gone flat—Billy Topsail was burning the fragments of the komatik. All day the dogs had roamed the pan. They had not ventured near Billy Topsail's authority—not within reach of Billy's treacherously minded flattery and coaxing. In the exercise of this new freedom they had run wild and fought among themselves like a mutinous pirate crew. Now, however, with night down, they had crept out of its seclusion and were sitting on the edge of the firelight, staring, silent, pondering.

Teddy Brisk was tied up in the wolfskin bag. It was the best refuge for the lad. In the event of a rush he would not be torn in the scuffle; and should the dogs overcome Billy Topsail—which was not yet probable—the little boy would be none the worse off in the bag.

Had the dogs been a pack of wolves Billy would have been in livid fear of them ; but these beasts were dogs of his own harbour, which he had commanded at will and beaten at will, and he was awaiting the onset with grim satisfaction. In the end, as he knew, the dogs would have an advantage that could not be resisted ; but now—Billy Topsail would "l'arn 'em! Let 'em come!"

Billy's club, torn from the komatik, was lying one end in his little fire. He nursed it with care.

Cracker fawned up. In the shadows, behind, the pack stared attentive. It was a pretense at playfulness—Cracker's advance. Cracker pawed the ice, and wagged his tail, and laughed. This amused Billy. It was transparent cunning. Billy gripped his club and let the fire freely ignite the end of it. He was as keen as the dog—as sly and as alert.

He said :

"Good ol' dog!"

Obviously the man was not suspicious. Cracker's confidence increased. He moved quickly, then, within leaping distance. For a flash he paused, king-hairs rising. When he rushed, the pack failed him. It started, quivered, stopped, and cautiously stood still. Billy was up. The lift of Cracker's crest and the dog's taut pause had amply warned him.

A moment later Cracker was in scared, yelping flight from the pain and horror of Billy's blazing club, and the pack was in ravenous chase of him. Billy Topsail listened for the issue of the chase. It came presently—the confusion of a dog fight; and it was soon over. Cracker was either dead or master again. Billy hoped the pack had made an end of him and would be content. He could not be sure of the outcome. Cracker was a difficult beast.

Released from the wolfskin bag and heartened by Billy's laughter, Teddy Brisk demanded:

"Was it Cracker?"

"It was."

Teddy grinned.

"Did you fetch un a fatal wallop?"

"I left the dogs t' finish the job. Hark! They're not feastin', is they? Mm-m? I don't know."

They snuggled up to the little fire. Teddy Brisk was wistful. He talked now—as often before—of the coming of a skiff from Our Harbour. He had a child's intimate knowledge of his own mother—and a child's wise and abounding faith.

"I knows my mother's ways," he declared. "Mark me, Billy, my mother's an anxious woman an' wonderful fond o' me. When my mother heard that sou'west wind blow up, 'Skipper Thomas,' says she t' my grandfather, 'them b'ys is goin' out with the ice; an' you get right straight up out o' bed an' tend t' things.'

"An' my grandfather's a man; an' he says:

"'Go to, woman! They're ashore on Ginger Head long ago!'

"An' my mother says:

"'Ah, well, they mightn't be, you dunderhead!'—for she've a wonderful temper when she's afeared for my safety.

"An' my grandfather says:

"'They is, though.'

"An' my mother says:

"'You'll be off in the bait skiff t'-morrow, sir, with a flea in your ear, t' find out at Our Harbour.'

"An' she'd give that man his tea in a mug (scolding) until he got a Tight Cove crew t'gether an' put out across the bay. Ecod! but they'd fly across the bay in a gale o' wind like that! Eh, Billy?"

"All in a smother—eh, Teddy?"

"Yep—all in a smother. My grandfather's fit an' able for anything in a boat. An' they'd send the news up an' down the coast from Our Harbour—wouldn't they, Billy?"

"'Way up an' down the coast, Teddy."

"Yep—'way up an' down. They must be skiffs from Walk Harbour an' Skeleton Cove an' Come-Again Bight searchin' this floe for we—eh, Billy?"

"An' Our Harbour too."

"Yep—an' Our Harbour too. Jus' the way they done when ol' Bad-Weather West was cast away—eh, Billy? Don't you 'low so?"

"Jus' that clever way, Teddy."

"I reckon my mother'll tend t' that." Teddy's heart failed him then. "Anyhow, Billy," said he weakly, "you'll take care o' me—won't you—if the worst comes t' the worst?"

The boy was not too young for a vision of the worst coming to the worst.

"None better!" Billy replied.

"I been thinkin' I isn't very much of a man, Billy. I've not much courage left."

"Huh!" Billy scoffed. "When we gets ashore, an' I tells my tale o' these days ——"

Teddy started.

"Billy," said he, "you'll not tell what I said?"

"What was that now?"

"Jus' now, Billy—about ——"

"I heard no boast. An I was you, Teddy, I wouldn't boast too much. I'd cling t' modesty."

"I takes it back," said Teddy. He sighed. "An' I'll stand by."

It did not appear to Billy Topsail how this guardianship of the boy was to be accomplished. Being prolonged, it was a battle, of course, no man could win. The dogs were beaten off for the time. They would return—not that night, perhaps, or in the broad light of the next day; but in the dark of the night to come they would return, and, failing success then, in the dark of the night after.

That was the way of it.

CHAPTER VIII

In Which Teddy Brisk Escapes From the Wolf-skin Bag and Determines to Use His Crutch and Billy Topsail Comes to the Conclusion that "It Looks Bad"

NEXT day the dogs hung close. They were now almost desperately ravenous. It was agony for them to be so near the satisfaction of their hunger and in inhibitive terror of seizing it. Their mouths dripped. They were in torture—they whimpered and ran restless circles; but they did not dare. They would attack when the quarry was weak or unaware. Occasionally Billy Topsail sallied on them with his club and a loud, intimidating tongue, to disclose his strength and teach them discretion; and the dogs were impressed and restrained by this show. If Billy Topsail could catch and kill a dog he would throw the carcass to the pack and thus stave off attack. Having been fed, the dogs would be in a mild humour. Billy might then entice and kill another—for himself and Teddy Brisk.

THE DOGS WERE DESPERATELY RAVENOUS

Cracker was alive and still masterful. Billy went out in chase of Smoke. It was futile. Billy cut a ridiculous figure in the pursuit. He could neither catch the dog nor overreach him with blandishments; and a cry of alarm from the boy brought him back to his base in haste to drive off Cracker and Tucker and Sling, who were up to the wolf's trick of flanking. The dogs had reverted. They were wolves again—as nearly as harbour dogs may be. Billy perceived that they could no longer be dealt with as the bond dogs of Tight Cove.

In the afternoon Billy slept. He would need to keep watch through the night.

Billy Topsail had husbanded the fragments of the komatik. A fire burned all that night—a mere glow and flicker of light. It was the last of the wood. All that remained was the man's club and the boy's crutch. Now, too, the last of the food went. There was nothing to eat. What Billy had brought, the abundant provision of a picnic, with something for emergencies—the bread and tea and molasses—had been conserved, to be sure, and even attenuated. There was neither a crumb nor a drop of it left.

What confronted Billy Topsail now, however,

and alarmed his hope and courage, was neither wind nor frost, nor so much the inevitable pangs of starvation, which were not immediate, as a swift abatement of his strength. A starved man cannot long continue at bay with a club. Billy could beat off the dogs that night perhaps—after all, they were the dogs of Tight Cove, Cracker and Smoke and Tucker and Sling; but to-morrow night—he would not be so strong to-morrow night.

The dogs did not attack that night. Billy heard them close—the sniffing and whining and restless movement in the dark that lay beyond the light of his feeble fire and was accentuated by it. But that was all.

It was now clear weather and the dark of the moon. The day was bright and warm. When night fell again it was starlight—every star of them all twinkling its measure of pale light to the floe. The dogs were plain as shifting, shadowy creatures against the white field of ice. Billy Topsail fought twice that night. This was between midnight and dawn. There was no maneuvering. The dogs gathered openly, viciously, and delivered a direct attack. Billy beat them off. He was gasping and discouraged, though, at the end of the encounter. They would surely come again—and they did. They waited—an hour, it may have been; and then they came.

There was a division of the pack. Six dogs—Spunk and Biscuit and Hero in advance—rushed Billy Topsail. It was a reluctant assault. Billy disposed of the six—after all, they were dogs of Tight Cove, not wolves from the rigours of the timber; and Billy was then attracted to the rescue of Teddy Brisk, who was tied up in the wolfskin bag, by the boy's muffled screams. Cracker and Smoke and Tucker and Sling were worrying the wolfskin bag and dragging it off. They dropped it and took flight when Billy came roaring at them with a club.

When Billy released him from the wolfskin bag the boy was still screaming. He was not quieted—his cries and sobbing—until the day was broad.

"Gimme my crutch!" said he. "I'll never go in that bag no more!"

"Might as well wield your crutch," Billy agreed.

To survive another night was out of the question. Another night came in due course, however, and was to be faced.

It was a gray day. Sky and ice and fields of ruffled water had no warmth of colour. All the world was both cold and drear. A breeze was stirring down from the north and would be bitter in the dusk. It cut and disheartened the castaways. It portended, moreover, a black night.

Teddy cried a good deal that day—a little whimper, with tears. He was cold and hungry—the first agony of starvation—and frightened and homesick. Billy fancied that his spirit was broken. As for Billy himself, he watched the dogs, which watched him patiently near by—a hopeless vigil for the man, for the dogs were fast approaching a pass of need in which hunger would dominate the fear of a man with a club. And Billy was acutely aware of this much—that nothing but the habitual fear of a man with a club had hitherto restrained the full fury and strength of the pack.

That fury, breaking with determination, would be irresistible. No man could beat off the attack of ten dogs that were not, in the beginning, already defeated and overcome by awe of him.

In the dark—in the dark of that night Billy could easily be dragged down; and the dogs were manifestly waiting for the dark to fall.

It was to be the end.

"It looks bad—it do so, indeed!" Billy Topsail thought.

That was the full extent of his admission.

CHAPTER IX

In Which Attack is Threatened and Billy Topsail Strips Stark Naked in the Wind in Pursuit of a Desperate Expedient and with Small Chance of Success

TEDDY BRISK kept watch for a skiff from Our Harbour or Come-Again Bight. He depended for the inspiration of this rescue on his mother's anxious love and sagacity. She would leave nothing to the indifferent dealings and cold issue of chance; it was never "more by good luck than good conduct" with her, ecod!

"I knows my mother's ways!" he sobbed, and he repeated this many times as the gray day drew on and began to fail. "I tells you, Billy, I knows my mother's ways!"

And they were not yet beyond sight of the coast. Scotchman's Breakfast of Ginger Head was a wee white peak against the drab of the sky in the southwest; and the ragged line of cliffs running south and east was a long, thin ridge on the horizon where the cottages of Walk Harbour and Our Harbour were.

No sail fluttered between—a sail might be confused with the colour of the ice, however, or not yet risen into view; but by and by, when the misty white circle of the sun was dropping low, the boy gave up hope, without yielding altogether to despair. There would be no skiff along that day, said he; but there would surely be a sail to-morrow, never fear—Skipper Thomas and a Tight Cove crew.

In the light airs the floe had spread. There was more open water than there had been. Fragments of ice had broken from the first vast pans into which Schooner Bay ice had been split in the break-up. These lesser, lighter pans moved faster than the greater ones; and the wind from the north—blown up to a steady breeze by this time—was driving them slowly south against the windward edge of the more sluggish fields in that direction.

At sunset—the west was white and frosty—a small pan caught Billy Topsail's eye and instantly absorbed his attention. It had broken from the field on which they were marooned and was under way on a diagonal across a quiet lane of black water, towards a second great field lying fifty fathoms or somewhat less to the south.

Were Billy Topsail and the boy aboard that pan the wind would ferry them away from the horrible menace of the dogs. It was a small pan—an area of about four hundred square feet; yet it would serve. It was not more than fifteen fathoms distant. Billy could swim that far—he was pretty sure he could swim that far, the endeavour being unencumbered; but the boy—a little fellow and a cripple—could not swim at all.

Billy jumped up.

"We've got t' leave this pan," said he, "an' forthwith too."

"Have you a notion, b'y?"

Billy laid off his seal-hide overjacket. He gathered up the dogs' traces—long strips of seal leather by means of which the dogs had drawn the komatik, a strip to a dog; and he began to knot them together—talking fast the while to distract the boy from the incident of peculiar peril in the plan.

The little pan in the lane—said he—would be a clever ferry. He would swim out and crawl aboard. It would be no trick at all. He would carry one end of the seal-leather line. Teddy Brisk would retain the other. Billy pointed out a ridge of ice against which Teddy Brisk could brace his sound leg. They would pull, then—each against the other; and presently the little pan would approach and lie alongside the big pan—there was none too much wind for that—and they would board the little pan and push off, and drift away with the wind, and leave the dogs to make the best of a bad job.

It would be a slow affair, though—hauling in a pan like that; the light was failing too—flickering out like a candle end—and there must be courage and haste—or failure.

Teddy Brisk at once discovered the interval of danger to himself.

"I'll be left alone with the dogs!" he objected.

"Sure, b'y," Billy coaxed; "but then you see ——"

"I won't stay alone!" the boy sobbed. He shrank from the direction of the dogs towards Billy. At once the dogs attended. "I'm afeared t' stay alone!" he screamed. "No, no!"

"An we don't leave this pan," Billy scolded, "we'll be gobbled up in the night."

That was not the immediate danger. What confronted the boy was an immediate attack, which he must deal with alone.

"No! No! No!" the boy persisted.

"Ah, come now ——"

"That Cracker knows I'm a cripple, Billy. He'll turn at me. I can't keep un off."

Billy changed front.

"Who's skipper here?" he demanded.

"You is, sir."

"Is you takin' orders or isn't you?"

The effect of this was immediate. The boy stopped his clamour.

"I is, sir," said he.

"Then stand by!"

"Aye, sir!"—a sob and a sigh.

It was to be bitter cold work in the wind and water. Billy Topsail completed his preparations before he began to strip. He lashed the end of the seal-leather line round the boy's waist and put the club in his hand.

All this while he gave directions: The boy was to face the dogs; he was not to turn round for hints of Billy's progress or to be concerned at all with that; he was not to lose courage; he was to feint and scold ; he was to let no shadow of fear cross his face—no tremor of fear must touch his voice ; he was not to yield an inch ; he was not to sob and cover his eyes with his hands —in short, he was to mind his own task of keeping the dogs away and leave Billy to accomplish his.

And the boy answered : "Yes, sir!" and "Aye, sir!" and "Very well, sir!"—like an old hand of the coast.

It was stimulating. Billy Topsail was heartened. He determined privately that he would not turn to look back—that if the worst came to the worst, and he could manage to do so, he would jerk the lad into the water and let him drown. The snarling tumult of the onset would warn him when the worst had come to the worst.

And then he stripped stark naked, quickly stowed away his clothes in the midst of the boy's dogskin robes, tied the end of the seal-leather line round his waist, and ran to the edge of the pan.

"If you drowns——" the boy began.

"Keep them dogs off!" Billy Topsail roared. "I'll not drown!"

He slipped into the water and struck out.

CHAPTER X

In Which Teddy Brisk Confronts the Pack Alone and Cracker Leads the Assault

BY this time the sun was touching the cliffs of shore. It was a patch of struggling white light in the drear gray colour of the west. It would drop fast. In his punt, in summer weather, wondering all the while at the acceleration of this last descent, Teddy Brisk had often paused to watch the sun fall and flicker out of sight. It had seemed to fall beyond the rim of the world, like a ball.

"She tumbles through the last foot or two!" he had determined.

In a little while the sun would be gone. Now the sky was overcast and scowling. In the east it was already dusk. The cloudy black sky in the east caught no light from the feeble sun. Presently everywhere it would be dark. It had turned colder too. The wind from the north was still blowing up—a nipping gray wind which would sweep the floe and hamper the manipulation of the little pan towards which the naked Billy Topsail was striving.

And the wind lifted the dry snow and drove it past Teddy Brisk's feet in swirling wreaths. The floe was smoking, the boy thought. Before long the snow would rise higher and envelop him. And he thought that when Billy reached the little pan, and stood exposed and dripping in the blast, he would be very cold. It would take a long time, too, to haul the little pan across the lane of water.

It will be recalled that Teddy Brisk was ten years old. He stood alone. He knew the temper of the dogs. Billy Topsail was out of reach. The burden of fear had fallen on the boy—not on Billy. The boy had been in a panic; yet he was not now even afraid. Duty occupied him. He had no time for reflection. The hazard of the quarter of an hour to come, however, was clear to him. Should he fail to keep off the dogs through every moment of that time, he would be torn to death before Billy could return to his rescue.

Should Billy Topsail fail to reach the pan—should Billy go down midway—he would surely be devoured.

And Billy Topsail was no swimmer to boast of. Teddy knew that. He had heard Billy tell of it. Billy could keep afloat—could achieve a slow, splashing progress.

That was true. Billy's chance of winning the pan was small. But Teddy was Labrador born and bred. What now commanded his fear was Billy's orders to duty. Obedience to a skipper was laid on all men. It must be instant and unfailing in an emergency. Billy was in command. He was responsible. It was for the boy to obey. That was the teaching of his habitat.

Consequently Teddy Brisk's terror yielded and he stood fast.

When Billy began to strip, the dogs were disturbed. What was the man up to? What was this? Queer proceeding this! It was a trick. When he stood naked in the wind the dogs were uneasy. When he went into the water they were alarmed. They withdrew. Cracker and Smoke ran to the water's edge and stared at Billy—keeping half an eye on the boy meantime. It troubles a dog to see a man in the water. Smoke whined. Cracker growled and crouched to leap after Billy. He could easily overtake and drown Billy.

Teddy went at Cracker and Smoke with his club.

He screamed at them:

"Back, you, Cracker! Back, you, Smoke!"

The dogs responded to this furious authority. They scurried away and rejoined the others. Teddy taunted them. He laughed at the pack, challenged it—crutch under his left arm and club swinging in his right hand. He taunted the dogs by name—Cracker and Smoke and Tucker. This bewildered the dogs. They were infinitely suspicious. The boy hobbled at them in a rage, a few feet forth—the seal-leather line round his waist limited him—and defied them. They retreated.

When Teddy returned to the edge of the field they sat regarding him in amazement and renewed suspicion. In this way for a time the boy kept the dogs at a distance—by exciting their surprise and suspicion. It sufficed for a space. The dogs were curious. They were entertained. What was strange in the behaviour of the quarry, moreover, was fearsome to the dogs. It indicated unknown resources. The dogs waited.

Presently Teddy could devise no new startling gestures. He was never silent—he was never still; but his fantastic antics, growing familiar and proving innocuous, began to fail of effect. Something else—something out of the way and unexpected—must be done to distract and employ the attention of the dogs. They were aware of Billy Topsail's absence—they were cunning cowards and they would take advantage of the opportunity.

The dogs began to move—to whine and circle and toss their heads. Teddy could see the concerted purpose take form. It was as though they were conspiring together. He was fully aware of what impended. They were coming! he thought; and they were coming in a moment. It was an attack agreed on. They were to act as a pack.

They advanced. It was tentative and slow. They paused.

They came closer. Teddy brandished his club and reviled them in shrill screams. The dogs paused again. They crouched then. Cracker was in the lead. The boy hated Cracker. Cracker's white breast was touching the ice.

His head was thrust forward. His crest began to rise.

CHAPTER XI

In Which Teddy Brisk Gives the Strains of a Tight Cove Ballad to the North Wind, Billy Topsail Wins the Reward of Daring, Cracker Finds Himself in the Way of the Evil-Doer, and Teddy Brisk's Boast Makes Doctor Luke Laugh

STRIPPED down, at first, on the field, Billy Topsail would not yield to the cold. He did not shrink from the wind. He moved like a man all clothed. Nor would he yield to the shock of the water. He ignored it. It was heroic self-command. But he was the man for that—a Newfoundlander. He struck out precisely as though he had gone into the summer water of Ruddy Cove. If he relapsed from this attitude the cold would strike through him. A chill would momentarily paralyze his strength.

He was neither a strong nor a cunning swimmer. In this lapse he would go down and be choked beyond further effort before he could recover the use of his arms and legs. It was icy cold. He would not think of the cold. His best protection against it was the sufficient will to ignore it. The power would not long endure. It must endure until he had clambered out of the water to the little pan towards which he floundered. He was slow in the water. It seemed to him that his progress was mysteriously prolonged—that the wind was driving the pan away.

The wind could not rise to this pitch in a minute; but when he was midway of the lane he thought half an hour had elapsed—an hour—that he must have left the field and the boy far behind.

The boy was not much more than fifteen yards away.

A word of advice occurred to Billy. He did not turn. He was then within a dozen strokes of the little pan.

He shouted:

"Give un a tune!"

Teddy Brisk dropped his crutch, fumbled in his waistcoat pocket, whipped out his mouth organ, clapped it to his lips, and blew a lively air:

> Lukie's boat was painted green,
> The finest boat that ever was seen;
> Lukie's boat had cotton sails,
> A juniper rudder and galvanized nails.

And he so profoundly astonished the dogs with these sudden, harmonious sounds, accompanied by the jerky movement of a crippled leg, designed to resemble a dance, and in itself shockingly suspicious—so profoundly astonished the dogs that they paused to reconsider the matter in hand.

It was startling. They sat up. Aha! What was this? What did it portend?

And the little boy wheezed away:

> Lukie sailed her out one day,
> A fine spell o' weather in the month o' May;
> She leaked so bad when he put about,
> He drove her ashore on the Tailor's Snout.

And he kept on blowing that famous jig-time ballad of Tight Cove for dear life until a tug at the line round his waist warned him to brace himself against the steady pull to follow.

Teddy was still giving the strains of Lukie's adventure to the north wind when the little pan came alongside.

"Carry on!" Billy Topsail chattered behind him.

Teddy interrupted himself to answer:

"Aye, sir!"

"I'll get my clothes an' the skins aboard. Ecod! It's awful cold!"

Presently they pushed out from the field. It had not taken long. The patch of white light that was the sun had not yet dropped out of sight behind the cliffs of the shore.

It was a bad night on the field to the south. The boys were hungry. It was cold. Billy Topsail suffered from the cold. In the morning the northerly wind had turned the heap of dog-skin robes into a snowdrift. The sun shone. Billy was still cold. He shivered and chattered. He despaired. Rescue came, however, in the afternoon. It was the Tight Cove skiff, hailing now from Our Harbour, with Doctor Luke aboard.

The skiff from Come-Again Bight found the dogs. The dogs were wild—the men said—and would not come aboard, but ran off in a pack to the farthest limits of the field and were not seen again—save only Cracker, who fawned and jumped into the skiff without so much as a by-your-leave. And Cracker, in due course and according to custom, they hanged by the neck at Tight Cove until he was dead.

That day, however—the afternoon of the rescue—when the Tight Cove skiff came near, Teddy Brisk put his hands to his mouth and shouted—none too lustily:

"Ahoy!"

"Aye?" Skipper Thomas answered.

"Did my mother send you?"

"She did."

Teddy Brisk turned to Billy Topsail.

"Didn't I tell you," he sobbed, his eyes blazing, "that I knowed my mother's ways?"

And Doctor Luke laughed.

CHAPTER XII

In Which Billy Topsail's Agreeable Qualities Win a Warm Welcome with Doctor Luke at Our Harbour, There is an Explosion at Ragged Run, Tommy West Drops Through the Ice and Vanishes, and Doctor Luke is in a Way Never to Be Warned of the Desperate Need of His Services

IN Doctor Luke's little hospital at Our Harbour, Billy Topsail fell in with a charming group—Doctor Luke and his friends; and being himself a boy of a good many attractive qualities, and of natural good manners, which association with his friend Archie Armstrong, of St. John's, Sir Archibald's son, had helped to fashion—being a manly, good-mannered, humorous fellow, he was very soon warmly accepted. There was no mystery about Doctor Luke. He was an Englishman—a well-bred, cultured man; and having been wrecked on the coast, and having perceived the great need of a physician in those parts, he had thrown in his lot for good and all with the Labrador folk. And he was obviously happy—both busy and happy. That he regretted his determination was a preposterous thing to assume; on the contrary, he positively did not regret it—he whistled and sang and laughed and laboured, and Billy Topsail was convinced that he was not only the most useful man in the world, but the most delightful and best, and the happiest, too.

That Doctor Luke was useful was very soon evident to an astonishing degree. Teddy Brisk's leg was scraped—it was eventually healed and became quite as sound as Billy Topsail's "off shank." But there was a period of convalescence, during which Billy Topsail had all the opportunity in the world to observe just how mightily useful Doctor Luke was. The demands upon him were extraordinary; and his response to them—his ready, cheerful, skillful, brave response—was more extraordinary still.

Winter was not yet done with: summer delayed—there was more snow, more frost; and the ice drifted in and out with the variable winds: so that travelling in those parts was at its most dangerous period. Yet Doctor Luke went about with small regard for what might happen—afoot, with the dogs, and in a punt, when the ice, having temporarily drifted away, left open water. Up and down the coast, near and far, always on the wing: that was Doctor Luke—the busiest, happiest, most useful man Billy Topsail had ever known.

And Billy Topsail was profoundly affected by all this beneficent activity. He wished to emulate it. This was a secret, to be sure; there was no reason for Billy Topsail to think that a fisherman's son like himself would ever be presented with the opportunity to "wield a knife" and be made master of the arts of healing—and consequently he said nothing about the growing ambition. But the ambition flourished.

When Doctor Luke returned from his professional calls with tales of illness cured and distress alleviated, and when Billy Topsail reflected that there would have been neither cure nor alleviation had it not been for Doctor Luke's skill and kindly heart, Billy Topsail wanted with all his strength to be about that selfsame business. And there was a good deal in the performance of it to appeal to a lad like Billy Topsail—the adventure of the thing: for Doctor Luke seldom counted the chances, when they seemed not too unreasonably against him, and when the need was urgent he did not count them at all.

Billy Topsail was just a little bit puzzled at first. Why should Doctor Luke do these things? There was no gain—no material gain worth considering; but it did not take Billy Topsail long to perceive that there was in fact great gain—far exceeding material gain: the satisfaction in doing a good deed for what Doctor Luke called "the love of God" and nothing else whatsoever. Doctor Luke was not attached to any Mission. His work was his own: his field was his own—nobody contributed to his activities; nobody helped him in any way. Yet his work was done in the spirit of the missionary; and that was what Billy Topsail liked about it—the masterful, generous, high-minded quality of it.

Being an honest, healthy lad, Billy Topsail set Doctor Luke in the hero's seat and began to worship, as no good boy could very well help doing; it was not long, indeed, before Doctor Luke had grown to be as great a hero as Sir Archibald Armstrong, Archie's father—and that is saying a good deal. In the lap of the future there lay some adventures in which

Billy Topsail and Archie Armstrong were to be concerned; but Billy Topsail was not aware of that.

Billy Topsail was neither a prophet nor the son of a prophet. Sometimes, however, he sighed:

"I wish Archie was here!"

And that wish was to come true.

Before Teddy Brisk was well enough to be sent home, something happened at Ragged Run Cove, which lay across Anxious Bight, near by the hospital at Our Harbour; and Doctor Luke and Billy Topsail were at once drawn into the consequences of the accident. It was March weather. There was sunshine and thaw. Anxious Bight was caught over with rotten ice from Ragged Run Cove to the heads of Our Harbour. A rumour of seals—a herd on the Arctic drift-ice offshore—had come in from the Spotted Horses. It inspired instant haste in all the cottages of Ragged Run—an eager, stumbling haste.

In Bad-Weather Tom West's wife's kitchen, somewhat after ten o'clock in the morning, in the midst of this hilarious scramble to be off to the floe, there was a flash and spit of fire, pale in the sunshine, and the clap of an explosion and the clatter of a sealing gun on the bare floor; and in the breathless, dead little interval, enduring between the appalling detonation and a man's groan of dismay and a woman's choke and scream of terror—in this shocked silence, Dolly West, Bad-Weather Tom's small maid, and Joe West's niece, stood swaying, wreathed in gray smoke, her little hands pressed tight to her eyes.

She was a pretty little creature—she had been a pretty little creature: there had been yellow curls, in the Labrador way—and rosy cheeks and grave blue eyes; but now of all this shy, fair loveliness——

"You've killed her!"

"Dear Lord—no!" cried Uncle Joe West, whose gun had exploded.

Dolly dropped her hands. She reached out, then, for something to grasp.

And she plainted:

"I ithn't dead, mother. I juth'—I juth' can't thee."

She extended her red hands.

"They're all wet!" she complained.

By this time the mother had the little girl gathered close in her arms.

She moaned:

"Doctor Luke—quick!"

Tommy West caught up his cap and mittens and sprang to the door.

"Not by the Bight!" Joe West shouted.

"No, sir."

Dolly West whimpered:

"It thmart-th, mother!"

"By Mad Harry an' Thank-the-Lord!"

"Ay, sir."

Dolly screamed—now:

"It hurt-th! Oh, oh, it hurt-th!"

"An' haste, lad!"

"Ay, sir."

There was of course no doctor at Ragged Run; there was a doctor, Doctor Luke, at Our Harbour, however—across Anxious Bight. Tommy West avoided the rotten ice of the Bight, which he dared not cross, and took the 'longshore trail by way of Mad Harry and Thank-the-Lord. At noon he was past Mad Harry, his little legs wearing well and his breath coming easily through his expanded nostrils—he had not paused; and at four o'clock—still on a dog-trot—he had hauled down the chimney smoke of Thank-the-Lord and was bearing up for Our Harbour. Early dusk caught him short-cutting the doubtful ice of Thank-the-Lord Cove; and half an hour later, midway of the passage to Our Harbour, with two miles left to accomplish—dusk falling thick and cold, then, and a frosty wind blowing—the heads of Our Harbour looming black and solid in the wintry night beyond—he dropped through the ice and vanished. There was not a sign of him left—some bubbles, perhaps: nothing more.

CHAPTER XIII

In Which Doctor Luke Undertakes a Feat of Daring and Endurance and Billy Topsail Thinks Himself the Luckiest Lad in the World

RETURNING from a call at Tumble Tickle, in clean, sunlit weather, with nothing more tedious than eighteen miles of wilderness trail and rough floe ice behind him, Doctor Luke was chagrined to discover himself a bit fagged. He had come heartily down the trail from Tumble Tickle in the early hours of that fine, windy morning, fit and eager for the trudge—as a matter of course; but on the ice, in the shank of the day—there had been eleven miles of the floe—he had lagged. A man cannot practice medicine out of a Labrador outport harbour and not know what it means to stomach a physical exhaustion. Doctor Luke had been tired before. He was not disturbed by that. But being human, he looked forward to rest; and in the drear, frosty dusk, when he rounded the heads of Home, opened the lights of Our Harbour, and caught the warm, yellow gleam of the lamp in the surgery window, he was glad to be near his supper and his bed.

And so he told Billy Topsail, whom he found in the surgery, replenishing the fire.

"Ha, Billy!" said he. "I'm glad to be home."

Afterwards, when supper had been disposed of, and Doctor Luke was with Billy in the surgery, the rest of the family being elsewhere occupied, there was a tap on the surgery door. Doctor Luke called: "Come in!"—with some wonder as to the event. It was no night to be abroad on the ice. Yet the tap on the surgery door could mean but one thing—somebody was in trouble; and as he called "Come in!" and while he waited for the door to open, Doctor Luke considered the night and wondered what strength he had left.

A youngster—he had been dripping wet and was now sparkling all over with frost and ice in the light of the surgery lamp—intruded.

"Thank-the-Lord Cove?"

"No, sir."

"Mad Harry?"

"Ragged Run, sir."

"Bad-Weather West's lad?"

"Yes, sir."

"Been in the water?"

The boy grinned. He was ashamed of himself. "Yes, sir. I falled through the ice, sir."

"Come across the Bight?"

The boy stared. "No, sir. A cat couldn't cross the Bight the night, sir. 'Tis all rotten. I come alongshore by Mad Harry an' Thank-the-Lord. I dropped through all of a sudden, sir, in Thank-the Lord Cove."

"Who's sick?"

"Uncle Joe's gun went off, sir."

Doctor Luke rose. "Uncle Joe's gun went off! Who was in the way?"

"Dolly, sir."

"And Dolly in the way! And Dolly ——"

"She've gone blind, sir. An' her cheek, sir—an' one ear, sir ——"

"What's the night?"

"Blowin' up, sir. There's a scud. An' the moon ——"

"You didn't cross the Bight? Why not?"

"'Tis rotten from shore t' shore. I'd not try the Bight, sir, the night."

"No?"

"No, sir." The boy was very grave.

"Mm-m."

All this while Doctor Luke had been moving about the surgery in sure haste—packing a waterproof case with little instruments and vials and what-not. And now he got quickly into his boots and jacket, pulled down his coonskin cap, pulled up his sealskin gloves, handed Bad-Weather West's boy over to the family for supper and bed, and was about to close the surgery door upon himself when Billy Topsail interrupted him.

"I say, sir!"

Doctor Luke halted.

"Well, Billy?"

"Take me, sir! Won't you?"

"What for?"

"I wants t' go."

"I go the short way, Billy."

"Sure, you does! I knows *you*, sir!"

Doctor Luke laughed.

"Come on!" said he.

Billy Topsail thought himself the luckiest lad in the world. And perhaps he was.

CHAPTER XIV

In Which Billy Topsail and Doctor Luke Take to the Ice in the Night and Doctor Luke Tells Billy Topsail Something Interesting About Skinflint Sam and Bad-Weather Tom West of Ragged Run

DOCTOR LUKE and Billy Topsail took to the harbour ice and drove head down into the gale. There were ten miles to go. It was to be a night's work. They settled themselves doggedly to the miles. It was a mile and a half to the Head, where the Tickle led a narrow way from the shelter of Our Harbour to Anxious Bight and the open sea; and from the lee of the Head—a straightaway across Anxious Bight—it was nine miles to Blow-me-Down Dick of Ragged Run Cove. Doctor Luke had rested but three hours. It was but a taste. Legs and feet were bitterly unwilling to forego a sufficient rest. They complained of the interruption. They were stiff and sore and sullen. It was hard to warm them to their labour. Impatient to revive the accustomed comfort and glow of strength, Doctor Luke began to run.

Presently they slowed up. Doctor Luke told Billy Topsail, as they pushed on, something about the Ragged Run family they were to visit. "There is a small trader at Ragged Run," said he. "A strange mixture of conscience and greed he is. Skinflint Sam—they call him. Conscience? Oh, yes, he has a conscience! And his conscience—as he calls it—has made him rich as riches go in these parts. No, of course not! You wouldn't expect a north-coast trader to have a conscience; and you wouldn't expect a north-coast trader with a conscience to be rich!"

Billy Topsail agreed with this.

"Ah, well," Doctor Luke went on, "conscience is much like the wind. It blows every which way (as they say); and if a man does but trim his sails to suit, he can bowl along in any direction without much wear and tear of the spirit. Skinflint Sam bowled along, paddle-punt fisherman to Ragged Run merchant. Skinflint went where he was bound for, wing-and-wing to the breeze behind, and got there with his peace of mind showing never a sign of the weather. It is said that the old man has an easy conscience and ten thousand dollars!

"This Bad-Weather West vowed long ago

that he would even scores with Skinflint Sam before he could pass to his last harbour with any satisfaction.

"'With me, Tom?' said Sam. 'That's a saucy notion for a hook-an'-line man.'

"'Ten more years o' life,' said Tom, 'an' I'll square scores.'

"'Afore you evens scores with me, Tom,' said Sam, 'you'll have t' have what I wants.'

"'I may have it.'

"'An' also,' said Sam, 'what I can't get.'

"'There's times,' said Tom, 'when a man stands in sore need o' what he never thought he'd want.'

"'When you haves what I needs,' said Sam, 'I'll pay what you asks.'

"'If 'tis for sale,' said Tom.

"'Money talks,' said Sam.

"'Ah, well,' said Tom, 'maybe it don't speak my language.'

"Of course, Skinflint Sam's conscience is just as busy as any other man's conscience. I think it troubles Sam. It doesn't trouble him to be honest, perhaps; it troubles him only to be rich. And possibly it gives him no rest. When trade is dull—no fish coming into Sam's storehouses and no goods going out of Sam's shop—Sam's conscience makes him grumble and groan. They say a man never was so tortured by conscience before.

"And to ease his conscience Sam goes over his ledgers by night; and he will jot down a gallon of molasses here, and a pound of tea there, until he has made a good day's trade of a bad one. 'Tis simple enough, too: for Sam gives out no accounts, but just strikes his balances to please his greed, at the end of the season, and tells his dealers how much they owe him or how little he owes them."

Doctor Luke paused.

"Ay," said Billy Topsail. "I've seed that way o' doin' business."

"We all have, Billy," said Doctor Luke. And resumed: "In dull times Sam's conscience irks him into overhauling his ledgers. 'Tis otherwise in seasons of plenty. But Sam's conscience apparently keeps pricking away just the same—aggravating Sam into getting richer and richer. There is no rest for Skinflint Sam. Skinflint Sam must have all the money he can take by hook and crook or suffer the tortures of an evil conscience. And as any other man, Sam must ease that conscience or lose sleep o' nights.

"And so in seasons of plenty up goes the price of tea at Skinflint Sam's shop. And up goes the price of pork. And up goes the price of flour. All sky high, ecod! Never was such harsh times (says Sam); why, my dear man, up St. John's way (says he) you couldn't touch tea nor pork nor flour with a ten-foot sealing-gaff. And no telling what the world is coming to, with prices soaring like a gull in a gale and all the St. John's merchants chary of credit!

"''Tis awful times for us poor traders,' says Sam. 'No tellin' who'll weather this here panic. I'd not be surprised if we got a war out of it.'

"Well, now, as you know, Billy, on the north-coast in these days it isn't much like the big world beyond. Folk don't cruise about. They are too busy. And they are not used to it any-how. Ragged Run folk are not born at Ragged Run, raised at Rickity Tickle, married at Sel-dom-Come-By, aged at Skeleton Harbour and buried at Run-By-Guess. They are born and buried at Ragged Run. So what the fathers think at Ragged Run, the sons think; and what the sons know, has been known by the old men for a good many years.

"Nobody is used to changes. They are shy

of changes. New ways are fearsome. And so the price of flour is a mystery. *It is, anyhow.* Why it should go up and down at Ragged Run is beyond any man of Ragged Run to fathom. When Skinflint Sam says that the price of flour is up—well, then, it is up; and that's all there is about it. Nobody knows better. And Skinflint Sam has the flour. You know all about that sort of thing, don't you, Billy?"

"Ay, sir," Billy replied. "But I been helpin' the clerk of an honest trader."

"There are honest traders. Of course! Not Sam, though. And, as I was saying, Sam has the pork, as well as the flour. And he has the sweetness and the tea. And he has the shoes and the clothes and the patent medicines. And he has the twine and the salt. And he has almost all the cash there is at Ragged Run. And he has the schooner that brings in the supplies and carries away the fish to the St. John's markets.

"He is the only trader at Ragged Run. His storehouses and shop are jammed with the things that the folk of Ragged Run can't do without and are able to get nowhere else. So all in all, Skinflint Sam can make trouble for the folk that make trouble for him. And the folk grumble. But it is all they have the courage to do. And Skinflint Sam lets them grumble away. The best cure for grumbling (says he) is to give it free course. If a man can speak out in meeting (says he) he will work no mischief in secret.

"'Sea-lawyers, eh?' says Sam. 'Huh! What you fellers want, anyhow? Huh? You got everything now that any man could expect. Isn't you housed? Isn't you fed? Isn't you clothed? Isn't you got a parson and a schoolmaster? I believes you wants a doctor settled in the harbour! A doctor! An' 'tisn't two years since I got you your schoolmaster! Queer times we're havin' in the outports these days with every harbour on the coast wantin' a doctor within hail.

"'You're well enough done by at Ragged Run. None better nowhere. An' why? Does you ever think o' that? Why? Because I got my trade here. An' think o' *me!* If ar a one o' you had my brain-labour t' do, you'd soon find out what harsh labour was like. What with bad debts, an' roguery, an' failed seasons, an' creditors t' St. John's, I'm hard put to it t' keep my seven senses. An' small thanks I gets—me that keeps this harbour alive in famine an' plenty. 'Tis the business I haves that keeps you. You make trouble for my business, an' you'll come t' starvation! Now, you mark me!'

"I do not want you to think too harshly of Skinflint Sam. No doubt he has his good points. Most of us can discover a good point or two in ourselves and almost everybody else. There are times when Skinflint Sam will yield an inch. Oh, yes! I've known Skinflint Sam to drop the price of stick-candy when he had put the price of flour too high for anybody's comfort."

CHAPTER XV

In Which Bad-Weather Tom West's Curious Financial Predicament is Explained

"WELL, now," said Doctor Luke, continuing his tale, "Bad-Weather Tom West, of Ragged Run, has a conscience, too. But 'tis just a common conscience. Most men have that kind. It is not like Skinflint Sam's conscience. Nothing 'useful' ever comes of it. It is like yours and mine, Billy. It troubles Tom West to be honest and it keeps him poor. All Tom West's conscience ever aggravates him to do"—Doctor Luke was speaking in gentle irony now—"is just to live along in a religious sort of fashion, and rear his family, and be decently stowed away in the graveyard when his time is up if the sea doesn't catch him first.

"But 'tis a busy conscience for all that—and as sharp as a fish-prong. There is no rest for Tom West if he doesn't fatten his wife and crew of little lads and maids. There is no peace of mind for Tom if he doesn't labour! And so

Tom labours, and labours, and labours. Dawn to dusk, in season, his punt is on the grounds off Lack-a-Day Head, taking fish from the sea to be salted and dried and passed into Skinflint Sam's storehouses.

"The tale began long ago, Billy. When Tom West was about fourteen years old, his father died. 'Twas of a Sunday afternoon, Tom says, that they stowed him away. He remembers the time: spring weather and a fair day, with the sun low, and the birds twittering in the alders just before turning in.

"Skinflint Sam caught up with young Tom on the road home from the little graveyard on Sunset Hill.

"'Well, lad,' said he, 'the old skipper's gone.'

"'Ay, sir, he's dead an' buried.'

"'A fine man,' said Skinflint. 'None finer.'

"With that young Tom broke out crying: 'He were a kind father t' we,' says he. 'An' now he's dead!'

"'You lacked nothin' in your father's lifetime,' said Sam.

"'An' now he's dead!'

"'Well, well, you've no call t' be afeared o' goin' hungry on that account,' said Sam, putting an arm over the lad's shoulder. 'No; nor none o' the little crew over t' your house. Take up the fishin' where your father left it off, lad,' said he, 'an' you'll find small difference. I'll cross out your father's name on the books an' put down your own in its stead.'"

Billy Topsail interrupted.

"That was kind!" he snorted, in anger. "What a kind man this Skinflint is!"

And Doctor Luke continued:

"'I'm fair obliged,' said Tom. 'That's kind, sir.'

"'Nothin' like kindness t' ease sorrow,' said Skinflint Sam. 'Your father died in debt, lad.'

"'Ay, sir?'

"'Deep.'

"'How much, sir?'

"'I'm not able t' tell offhand,' said Sam. ''Twas deep enough. But never you care. You'll be able t' square it in course o' time. You're young an' hearty. An' I'll not be harsh. *I'm* no skinflint!'

"'That's kind, sir.'

"'You—you—*will* square it?'

"'I don't know, sir.'

"'*What?*' cried Sam. '*What!* You're not

knowin', eh? That's saucy talk. Didn't you have them there supplies?'

"'I 'low, sir.'

"'An' you guzzled your share, I'll be bound!'

"'Yes, sir.'

"'An' your mother had her share?'

"'Yes, sir.'

"'An' you're not knowin' whether you'll pay or not! Ecod! What is you? A scoundrel? A dead beat? A rascal? A thief? A jail-bird?'

"'No, sir.'

"''Tis for the likes o' you that jails was made.'

"'Oh, no, sir!'

"'Doesn't you go t' church? Is that what they learns you there? I'm thinkin' the parson doesn't earn what I pays un. Isn't you got no conscience?'

"'Twas just a little too much for young Tom. You see, Tom West *had* a conscience—a conscience as fresh and as young as his years. And Tom had loved his father well. And Tom honoured his father's name. And so when he had brooded over Skinflint Sam's words for a time—and when he had lain awake in the night thinking of his father's goodness—he went over to Skinflint's office and said that he would pay his father's debt.

"Skinflint gave him a clap on the back.

"'You are an honest lad, Tom West!' said he. 'I knowed you was. I'm proud t' have your name on my books!'

"And after that Tom kept hacking away on his father's debt.

"In good years Skinflint would say:

"'She's comin' down, Tom. I'll just apply the surplus.'

"And in bad he'd say:

"'You isn't quite cotched up with your own self this season, b'y. A little less pork this season, Tom, an' you'll square this here little balance afore next. I wisht this whole harbour was as honest as you. No trouble, then,' said he, 't' do business in a businesslike way.'

"When Tom got over the hill—fifty and more—his father's debt, with interest, according to Skinflint's figures, which Tom had no learning to dispute, was more than it ever had been; and his own was as much as he ever could hope to pay. And by that time Skinflint Sam was rich and Bad-Weather Tom was gone sour. One of these days—and not long, now—I shall make it my business to settle with Skinflint Sam. And I should have done so before, had I known of it."

"When did you find out, sir?"

"Bad-Weather Tom," Doctor Luke replied, "came to consult me about two months ago. He is in a bad way. I—well, I had to tell him so. And then he told me what I have told you—all about Skinflint Sam and his dealings with him. It was an old story, Billy. I have—well, attended to such matters before, in my own poor way. Bad-Weather Tom did not want me to take this up. 'You leave it to me,' said he; 'an' I'll fix it meself.' I wish he might be able to 'fix' it to his satisfaction."

"I hopes he does!" said Billy.

"Well, well," Doctor Luke replied, "it is Bad-Weather Tom's maid who is in need of us at Ragged Run."

Billy liked that "Us"!

CHAPTER XVI

In Which Doctor Luke and Billy Topsail Proceed to Accomplish What a Cat Would Never Attempt and Doctor Luke Looks for a Broken Back Whilst Billy Topsail Shouts, "Can You Make It?" and Hears No Answer

WHEN they came to the Head and there paused to survey Anxious Bight in a flash of the moon Billy Topsail and Doctor Luke were tingling and warm and limber and eager. Yet they were dismayed by the prospect. No man could cross from the Head to Blow-me-Down Dick of Ragged Run Cove in the dark. Doctor Luke considered the light. Communicating masses of ragged cloud were driving low across Anxious Bight. Offshore there was a sluggish bank of black cloud. And Doctor Luke was afraid of that bank of black cloud. The moon was risen and full. It was obscured. The intervals of light were less than the intervals of shadow. Sometimes a wide, impenetrable cloud, its edges alight, darkened the moon altogether. Still—there was light enough. All that was definitely ominous was the bank of black cloud lying sluggishly off-shore.

"I don't like that cloud, Billy," said Doctor Luke.

"No, sir; no more does I."

"It will cover the moon by and by."

"Sure, sir."

"There may be snow in it."

"Sure t' be, sir."

The longer Doctor Luke contemplated that bank of black cloud—its potentiality for catastrophe—the more he feared it.

"If we were to be overtaken by snow ——"

Billy interrupted with a chuckle.

"'Twould be a tidy little fix," said he. "Eh, sir?"

"Well, if that's all you have to say," said Doctor Luke—and he laughed—"come right along!"

It was blowing high. There was the bite and shiver of frost in the wind. Half a gale ran in from the open sea. Midway of Anxious Bight it would be a saucy, hampering, stinging head-wind. And beyond the Head the ice was in doubtful condition. A man might conjecture: that was all. What was it Tommy West had said? "A cat couldn't cross!" It was mid-spring. Freezing weather had of late alternated with periods of thaw and rain. There had been windy days. Anxious Bight had even once been clear of ice. A westerly wind had broken the ice and swept it out beyond the heads; a punt had fluttered over from Ragged Run Cove.

In a gale from the northeast, however, these fragments had returned with accumulations of Arctic pans and hummocks from the Labrador Current; and a frosty night had caught them together and sealed them to the cliffs of the coast. It was a slender attachment—a most delicate attachment: one pan to the other and the whole to the rocks.

It had yielded somewhat—it must have gone rotten—in the weather of that day.

What the frost had accomplished since dusk could be determined only upon trial.

"Soft as cheese!" Doctor Luke concluded.

"Rubber ice," said Billy.

"Air-holes," said the Doctor.

There was another way to Ragged Run—the way by which Tommy West had come. It skirted the shore of Anxious Bight—Mad Harry and Thank-the-Lord and Little Harbour Deep—

and something more than multiplied the distance by one and a half. Doctor Luke was completely aware of the difficulties of Anxious Bight, and so was Billy Topsail—the way from Our Harbour to Ragged Run: the treacherous reaches of young ice, bending under the weight of a man, and the veiled black water, and the labour, the crevices, the snow-crust of the Arctic pans and hummocks, and the broken field and wash of the sea beyond the lesser island of the Spotted Horses.

They knew, too, the issue of the disappearance of the moon—the desperate plight into which the sluggish bank of black cloud might plunge a man

Yet they now moved out and shaped a course for the black bulk of the Spotted Horses.

This was in the direction of Blow-me-Down Dick of Ragged Run and the open sea.

"Come on!" said Doctor Luke.

"I'm comin', sir," Billy replied.

There was something between a chuckle and a laugh from Billy's direction.

Doctor Luke started.

"Laughing, Billy?" he inquired.

"I jus' can't help it, sir."

"Nothing much to laugh at."

"No, sir," Billy replied. "I don't *feel* like laughin', sir. But 'tis so wonderful dangerous out on the Bight that I jus' can't *help* laughin'."

Doctor Luke and Billy Topsail were used to travelling all sorts of ice in all sorts of weather. The returning fragments of the ice of Anxious Bight had been close packed for two miles beyond the entrance to Our Harbour by the northeast gale that had driven them back from the open. An alien would have stumbled helplessly and exhausted himself; by and by he would have begun to crawl—in the end he would have lost his life in the frost. This was rough ice. In the press of the wind the drifting floe had buckled. It had been a big gale. Under the whip of it, the ice had come down with a rush. And when it encountered the coast, the first great pans had been thrust out of the sea by the weight of the floe behind.

A slow pressure had even driven them up the cliffs of the Head and heaped them in a tumble below.

It was thus a folded, crumpled floe—a vast field of broken bergs and pans at angles.

No Newfoundlander would adventure on the ice without a gaff. A gaff is a lithe, iron-shod pole, eight or ten feet in length. Doctor Luke was as cunning and sure with the gaff as any old hand of the sealing fleet; and Billy Topsail always maintained that he had been born with a little gaff in his hand instead of a silver spoon in his mouth. They employed the gaffs now to advantage. They used them like vaulting poles. They walked less than they leaped. But this was no work for the half-light of an obscured moon. Sometimes they halted for light. And delay annoyed Doctor Luke. A peppery humour began to possess him. A pause of ten minutes—they squatted for rest meantime—threw him into a state of incautious irritability. At this rate it would be past dawn before they made the cottages of Ragged Run Cove.

It would be slow beyond—surely slow on the treacherous reaches of green ice between the floe and the Spotted Horses.

And beyond the Spotted Horses, whence the path to Ragged Run led—the crossing of Tickle-my-Ribs!

A proverb of Our Harbour maintains that a fool and his life are soon parted.

Doctor Luke invented the saying.

"'Twould be engraved on my stationery," he would declare, out of temper with recklessness, "if I had any engraved stationery!"

Yet now, impatient of precaution, when he thought of Dolly West, Doctor Luke presently chanced a leap. It was error. As the meager light disclosed the path, a chasm of fifteen feet intervened between the edge of the upturned pan upon which he and Billy Topsail stood and a flat-topped hummock of Arctic ice to which he was bound. There was footing for the tip of his gaff midway below. He felt for this footing to entertain himself whilst the moon delayed.

It was there. He was tempted. It was an encouragement to rash conduct. The chasm was critically deep for the length of the gaff. Worse than that, the hummock was higher than the pan. Doctor Luke peered across. It was not *much* higher. Was it too high? No. It would merely be necessary to lift stoutly at the climax of the leap. And there was need of haste—a little maid in hard case at Ragged Run and a rising cloud threatening black weather.

"Ah, sir, don't leap it!" Billy pleaded.

"Tut!" scoffed the Doctor.

"Wait for the moon, sir!"

A slow cloud covered the moon. It was aggravating. How long must a man wait? A man must take a chance—what? And all at once Doctor Luke gave way to impatience. He gripped his gaff with angry determination and projected himself towards the hummock of Arctic ice. In mid-air he was doubtful. A flash later he had regretted the hazard. It seemed he would come short of the hummock altogether. He would fall. There would be broken bones. He perceived now that he had misjudged the height of the hummock.

Had the gaff been a foot longer Doctor Luke would have cleared the chasm. It occurred to him that he would break his back and merit the fate of his callow mistake. Then his toes caught the edge of the flat-topped hummock. His boots were of soft seal-leather. He gripped the ice. And now he hung suspended and inert. The slender gaff bent under the prolonged strain of his weight and shook in response to the shiver of his arms.

Billy Topsail shouted:

"Can you make it, sir?"

There was no answer.

CHAPTER XVII

In Which Rubber Ice is Encountered and Billy Topsail is Asked a Pointed Question

DOLLY WEST'S mother, with Dolly in her arms, resting against her soft, ample bosom, sat by the kitchen fire. It was long after dark. The wind was up—the cottage shook in the squalls. She had long ago washed Dolly's eyes and temporarily staunched the terrifying flow of blood; and now she waited—and had been waiting, with Dolly in her arms, a long, long time; rocking gently and sometimes crooning a plaintive song of the coast to the restless child.

Uncle Joe West came in.

"Hush!"

"Is she sleepin' still?"

"Off an' on. She've a deal o' pain. She cries out, poor lamb!"

Dolly stirred and whimpered.

"Any sign of un, Joe?"

"'Tis not time."

"He might ——"

"'Twill be hours afore he comes. I'm jus' wonderin' ——"

"Hush!"

Dolly moaned.

"Ay, Joe?"

"Tommy's but a wee feller. I'm wonderin' if he ——"

The woman was confident. "He'll make it," she whispered.

"Ay; but if he's delayed ——"

"He was there afore dusk. An' Doctor Luke got underway across the Bight ——"

"He'll not come by the Bight!"

"He'll come by the Bight. I knows that man. He'll come by the Bight—an' he'll ——"

"Pray not!"

"I pray so."

"If he comes by the Bight, he'll never get here at all. The Bight's breakin' up. There's rotten ice beyond the Spotted Horses. An' Tickle-my-Ribs is ——"

"He'll come. He'll be here afore ——"

"There's a gale o' snow comin' down. 'Twill cloud the moon. A man would lose hisself ——"

"He'll come."

Uncle Joe West went out again. This was

to plod once more down the narrows to the base of Blow-me-Down Dick and search the vague light of the coast towards Thank-the-Lord and Mad Harry for the first sight of Doctor Luke. It was not time. He knew that. There would be hours of waiting. It would be dawn before a man could come by Thank-the-Lord and Mad Harry if he left Our Harbour even so early as dusk. And as for crossing the Bight—no man could cross the Bight. It was blowing up, too—clouds rising and a threat of snow abroad. Uncle Joe West glanced apprehensively towards the northeast. It would snow before dawn. The moon was doomed. A dark night would fall.

And the Bight—Doctor Luke would never attempt to cross the Bight——

Doctor Luke, hanging between the hummock and the pan, the gaff shivering under his weight, slowly subsided towards the hummock. It was a slow, cautious approach. He had no faith in his foothold. A toe slipped. He paused. It was a grim business. The other foot held. The leg, too, was equal to the strain. He wriggled his toe back to its grip of the edge of the ice. It was an improved foothold. He turned then and began to lift and thrust himself backward. And a last thrust on the gaff set him on his haunches on the Arctic hummock.

He turned to Billy Topsail.

"Thank God!" said he. And then: "Come on, Billy!"

There was a better light now. Billy Topsail chose a narrower space to leap. And he leaped it safely. And they went on; and on—and on! There was a deal of slippery crawling to do—of slow, ticklish climbing. Doctor Luke and Billy Topsail rounded bergs, scaled perilous inclines, leaped crevices. Sometimes they were bewildered for a space. When the moon broke they could glimpse the Spotted Horses from the highest elevations of the floe. In the depressions of the floe they could not descry the way at all.

It was as cold as death now. Was it ten below? The gale bit like twenty below.

"'*Tis* twenty below!" Billy Topsail insisted.

Doctor Luke ignored this.

"We're near past the rough ice," said he, gravely.

"Rubber ice ahead," said Billy.

Neither laughed.

"Ay," the Doctor observed; and that was all.

When the big northeast wind drove the ice back into Anxious Bight and heaped it inshore, the pressure had decreased as the mass of the floe diminished in the direction of the sea. The outermost areas had not felt the impact. They had not folded—had not "raftered." There had been no convulsion offshore as inshore when the rocks of Afternoon Coast interrupted the rush. The pans had come to a standstill and snuggled close.

When the wind failed they had subsided towards the open. As they say on the coast, the ice had "gone abroad." It was distributed. And after that the sea had fallen flat; and a vicious frost had caught the floe—wide-spread now—and frozen it fast. It was six miles from the edge of the raftered ice to the first island of the Spotted Horses. The flat pans were solid enough—safe and easy going; but this new, connecting ice—the lanes and reaches of it ——

Doctor Luke's succinct characterization of the condition of Anxious Bight was also keen.

These six miles were perilous.

"Soft as cheese!"

All that day the sun had fallen hot on the

young ice in which the scattered pans of the floe were frozen. Doctor Luke recalled that in the afternoon he had splashed through an occasional pool of shallow water on the floe between Tumble Tickle and the short-cut trail to Our Harbour. Certainly some of the wider patches of green ice had been weakened to the breaking point. Here and there they must have been eaten clear through. It occurred to Doctor Luke—contemplating an advance with distaste—that these holes were like open sores.

And by and by the first brief barrier of new ice confronted Doctor Luke and Billy Topsail. They must cross it. A black film—the colour of water in that light—bridged the way from one pan to another. Neither Doctor Luke nor Billy Topsail would touch it. They leaped it easily. A few fathoms forward a second space halted them. Must they put foot on it? With a running start a man could—well, they chose not to touch the second space, but to leap it.

Soon a third interval interrupted them. No man could leap it. Doctor Luke cast about for another way. There was none. He must run across. A flush of displeasure ran over him. He scowled. Disinclination increased.

"Green ice!" said he.

"Let me try it, sir!"

"No."

"Ay, sir! I'm lighter."

"No."

Billy Topsail crossed then like a cat before he could be stopped—on tiptoe and swiftly; and he came to the other side with his heart in a flutter.

"Whew!"

The ice had yielded without breaking. It had creaked, perhaps—nothing worse. Doctor Luke crossed the space without accident. It was what is called "rubber ice." There was more of it—there were miles of it. As yet the pans were close together. Always however the intervals increased. The nearer the open sea the more wide-spread was the floe. Beyond—hauling down the Spotted Horses, which lay in the open—the proportion of new ice would be vastly greater.

At a trot, for the time, over the pans, which were flat, and in delicate, mincing little spurts across the bending ice, Doctor Luke and Billy Topsail proceeded. In a confidence that was somewhat flushed—they had rested—Doctor

Luke went forward. And presently, midway of a lane of green ice, he heard a gurgle, as the ice bent under his weight. Water washed his boots. He had been on the lookout for holes. This hole he heard—the spurt and gurgle of it. He had not seen it.

"Back!" he shouted, in warning.

Billy ran back.

"All right, sir?"

Safe across, Doctor Luke grinned. It was a reaction of relief.

"Whew! *Whew!*" he whistled. "Try below."

Billy crossed below.

"Don't you think, sir," said he, doubtfully, "that we'd best go back?"

"Do you think so?"

Billy reflected.

"No, sir," said he, flushing.

"Neither do I. Come on."

CHAPTER XVIII

In Which Discretion Urges Doctor Luke to Lie Still in a Pool of Water

IT was a mean light—this intermittent moonlight: with the clouds slow and thick, and the ominous bank of black cloud rising all the while from the horizon. A man should go slow in a light like that! But Doctor Luke and Billy Topsail must make haste. And by and by they caught ear of the sea breaking under the wind beyond the Little Spotted Horse. They were nearing the limits of the ice. In full moonlight the whitecaps flashed news of a tumultuous open. A rumble and splash of breakers came down with the gale from the point of the island. It indicated that the sea was working in the passage between the Spotted Horses and Blow-me-Down Dick of the Ragged Run coast. The waves would run under the ice—would lift it and break it. In this way the sea would eat its way through the passage. It would destroy the young ice. It would break the pans to pieces and rub them to slush.

Doctor Luke and Billy Topsail must make the Little Spotted Horse and cross the passage between the island and the Ragged Run coast.

"Come on!" said the Doctor again.

Whatever the issue of haste, they must carry on and make the best of a bad job. Otherwise they would come to Tickle-my-Ribs, between the Little Spotted Horse and Blow-me-Down Dick of Ragged Run, and be marooned from the mainshore. And there was another reason. It was immediate and desperately urgent. As the sea was biting off the ice in Tickle-my-Ribs so too it was encroaching upon the body of the ice in Anxious Bight.

Anxious Bight was breaking up. The scale of its dissolution was gigantic. Acres of ice were wrenched from the field at a time and then broken up by the sea. What was the direction of this swift melting? It might take any direction. And a survey of the sky troubled Doctor Luke no less than Billy Topsail. All this while the light had diminished. It was failing still. It was failing faster. There was less of the moon. By and by it would be wholly obscured.

"If we're delayed," Doctor Luke declared, "we'll be caught by the dark."

"Hear that, sir!" Billy exclaimed.

They listened.

"Breaking up fast!" said the Doctor.

Again there was a splitting crash. Another great fragment of the ice had broken away.

"Come on!" cried Billy, in alarm.

At first prolonged intervals of moonlight had occurred. Masses of cloud had gone driving across a pale and faintly starlit sky. A new proportion was disclosed. Now the stars were brilliant in occasional patches of deep sky. A glimpse of the moon was rare. From the north-east the ominous bank of black cloud had risen nearly overhead. It would eventually curtain both stars and moon and make a thick black night of it.

A man would surely lose his life on the ice in thick weather—on one or other of the reaches of new ice. And thereabouts the areas of young ice were wider. They were also more tender. Thin ice is a proverb of peril and daring. To tiptoe across the yielding film of these dimly visible stretches was instantly and dreadfully dangerous. It was horrifying. A man took his life in his hand every time he left a pan.

Doctor Luke was not insensitive. Neither

was Billy Topsail. They began to sweat—not with labour, but with fear. When the ice bent under them, they gasped and held their breath. They were in livid terror of being dropped through into the sea. They were afraid to proceed—they dared not stand still; and they came each time to the solid refuge of a pan with breath drawn, teeth set, faces contorted, hands clenched—a shiver in the small of the back. This was more exhausting than the labour of the folded floe. Upon every occasion it was like escaping an abyss.

To achieve safety once, however, was not to win a final relief—it was merely to confront, in the same circumstances, a precisely similar peril. Neither Doctor Luke nor Billy Topsail was physically exhausted. Every muscle that they had was warm and alert. Yet they were weak. A repetition of suspense had unnerved them. A full hour of this and sometimes they chattered and shook in a nervous chill.

In the meantime they had approached the rocks of the Little Spotted Horse.

They rested a moment.

"Now for it, boy!" said the Doctor, then.

"Ay, ay, sir!"

"Sorry you came, Billy?"

Billy was a truthful boy—and no hero of the melodrama.

"I wisht we was across, sir," said he.

"So do I," the Doctor agreed. "Come," he added, heartily; "we'll *go* across!"

In the lee of the Little Spotted Horse the ice had gathered as in a back-current. It was close packed alongshore to the point of the island. Between this solidly frozen press of pans and the dissolving field in Anxious Bight there had been a lane of ruffled open water before the frost fell. It measured perhaps fifty yards. It was now black and still—sheeted with new ice which had been delayed in forming by the ripple of that exposed situation.

Doctor Luke and Billy Topsail had encountered nothing as doubtful. They paused on the brink. A long, thin line of solid pan-ice, ghostly white in the dusk beyond, was attached to the rocks of the Little Spotted Horse. It led all the way to Tickle-my-Ribs. They must make that line of solid ice. They must cross the wide lane of black, delicately frozen new ice that lay between and barred their way. And there was no way out of it.

Doctor Luke waited for the moon. When the light broke—a thin, transient gleam—he started.

"Wait," said he, "until I'm across."

A few fathoms forth the ice began to yield. A moment later Doctor Luke stopped short and recoiled. There was a hole—gaping wide and almost under his feet. He stopped. The water overflowed and the ice cracked. He must not stand still. To avoid a second hole he twisted violently to the right and almost plunged into a third opening. It seemed the ice was rotten from shore to shore.

And it was a long way across. Doctor Luke danced a zigzag towards the pan-ice under the cliffs—spurting forward and retreating and swerving. He did not pause. Had he paused he would have dropped through. When he was within two fathoms of the pan-ice a foot broke through and tripped him flat on his face. With his weight thus distributed he was momentarily held up. Water squirted and gurgled out of the break—an inch of water, forming a pool.

Doctor Luke lay still and expectant in this pool.

CHAPTER XIX

In Which Doctor Luke and Billy Topsail Hesitate in Fear on the Brink of Tickle-my-Ribs

DOLLY WEST'S mother still sat rocking by the kitchen fire. It was long past midnight now. Once more Uncle Joe West tiptoed in from the frosty night.

"Is she sleepin' still?" he whispered.

"Hush! She've jus' toppled off again. She's havin' a deal o' pain, Joe. An' she've been bleedin' again."

"Put her down on the bed, dear."

The woman shook her head. "I'm afeared 'twould start the wounds, Joe. I'm not wantin' t' start un again. Any sign o' Doctor Luke yet, Joe?"

"Not yet."

"He'll come soon."

"No; 'tis not near time. 'Twill be dawn afore he ——"

"Soon, Joe."

"He'll be delayed by snow. The moon's

near gone. 'Twill be black dark in half an hour. I felt a flake o' snow as I come in. An' he'll maybe wait at Mad Harry ——"

"He's comin' by the Bight, Joe."

Dolly stirred—cried out—awakened with a start—and lifted her bandaged head a little.

She did not open her eyes.

"Is that you, Doctor Luke, sir?" she plainted.

"Hush!" the mother whispered. "'Tis not the Doctor yet."

"When ——"

"He's comin'."

"I'll take a look," said Joe.

He went out again and stumbled down the path to Blow-me-Down Dick by Tickle-my-Ribs.

Doctor Luke lay still and expectant in the pool of water near the pan-ice and rocks of the Little Spotted Horse. He waited. Nothing happened. It was encouraging. But he did not dare stand up. Nor would he dare to get to his knees and crawl.

There was no help to be had from the agonized Billy Topsail.

Both knew it.

"Shall I come, sir?" Billy called.

"Stay where you are," Doctor Luke replied, "or we'll both drop through. Don't move."

"Ay, sir."

Presently Doctor Luke ventured delicately to take off a mitten—to extend his hand, to sink his finger-nails in the ice and attempt to draw himself forward. He tried again. It was a failure. His finger-nails were too short. He could merely scratch the ice. He reflected that if he did not concentrate his weight—that if he kept it distributed—he would not break through. And once more he tried to make use of his finger-nails.

There was no snow on this ice. It was a smooth, hard surface. It was dry. It turned out that the nails of the other hand were longer. Doctor Luke managed to gain half an inch before they slipped.

They slipped again—and again and again. It was hopeless. Doctor Luke lay still—pondering.

Billy Topsail's agony of anxiety increased.

"Is you safe, sir?"

"Stay where you are!"

"Ay, sir!"

Doctor Luke could not continue to lie still. Presently he would be frozen in the pool of water. In emergencies he was used to indulging in a simple philosophical reflection: A man can lose his life but once. Now he shot his gaff towards the pan-ice, to be rid of the incumbrance of it, and lifted himself on his palms and toes. By this the distribution of his weight was not greatly disturbed. It was not concentrated upon one point. It was divided by four and laid upon four points.

And there were no fearsome consequences. It was a hopeful experiment. Doctor Luke stepped by inches on his hands towards the pan-ice—dragging his toes. In this way he came to the line of solid ice under the cliffs of the Little Spotted Horse and gained the refuge of it. And then he directed the crossing of Billy Topsail, who was much lighter, and crossed safely. Whereupon they set out for the point of the Little Spotted Horse and the passage of Tickle-my-Ribs. And they were heartened.

A country physician might say of a muddy, midnight call, in the wind and dark of a wet night in the fall of the year, that the roads were bad. Doctor Luke would have said of the way from Our Harbour to the Little Spotted Horse that he had been "in a bit of a mess." Thus far there had been nothing extravagantly uncommon in the night's experience. Doctor Luke and Billy Topsail had merely encountered and survived the familiar difficulties of a passage of Anxious Bight in a period of critical weather in the spring of the year.

A folded floe and six miles of rubber ice were not sufficiently out of the way to constitute an impressive incident. Doctor Luke had fared better and worse in his time. So had Billy Topsail. All this was not a climax. It was something to be forgotten in a confusion of experiences of the same description. It would not remain very long in the memory of either. In what lay ahead, however—the passage of Tickle-my-Ribs—there was doubtless an adventure.

"She'll be heavin' in this wind," Billy Topsail said.

"We'll get across," Doctor Luke replied, confidently. "Come along!"

Tickle-my-Ribs was heaving. The sea had by this time eaten its way clear through the passage from the open to the first reaches of Anxious

Bight and far and wide beyond. The channel was half a mile long—in width a quarter of a mile at the narrowest. Doctor Luke's path was determined. It must lead from the point of the island to the base of Blow-me-Down Dick and the adjoining fixed and solid ice of the narrows to Ragged Run Harbour. And ice choked the channel loosely from shore to shore.

It was a thin sheet of fragments—running through from the open. There was only an occasional considerable pan. A high sea ran outside. Waves from the open slipped under this field of little pieces and lifted it in running swells. In motion Tickle-my-Ribs resembled a vigorously shaken carpet. No single block of ice was at rest. The crossing would have been hazardous in the most favourable circumstances. And now aloft the moon and the ominous bank of black cloud had come close together.

Precisely as a country doctor might petulantly regard a stretch of hub-deep cross-road, Doctor Luke, the outport physician, when he came to the channel between the Little Spotted Horse and Blow-me-Down Dick of the Ragged Run coast, regarded the passage of Tickle-my-Ribs. Not many of the little pans would bear the weight of either himself or Billy Topsail. They would sustain it momentarily. Then they would tip or sink. There would be foothold only through the instant required to choose another foothold and leap towards it.

Always, moreover, the leap would have to be taken from sinking ground. When they came, by good chance, to a pan that would bear them up for a moment, they would have instantly to discover another heavy block to which to shape their agitated course. There would be no rest —no certainty beyond the impending moment. But leaping thus—alert and agile and daring—a man might——

Might? Mm-m—a man *might!* And he might *not!* There were contingencies. A man might leap short and find black water where he had depended upon a footing of ice—a man might land on the edge of a pan and fall slowly back for sheer lack of power to obtain a balance —a man might misjudge the strength of a pan to bear him up—a man might find no ice near enough for the next immediately imperative leap—a man might confront the appalling exigency of a lane of open water.

As a matter of fact, a man might be unable

either to go forward or retreat. A man might be submerged and find the shifting floe closed over his head. A man might easily lose his life in the driving, swelling rush of the shattered floe through Tickle-my-Ribs. And there was the light to consider. A man might be caught in the dark. He would be in hopeless case if caught in the dark. And the light might——

Light was imperative. Doctor Luke glanced aloft.

"Whew!" he whistled. "What do you think, Billy?"

Billy was flat.

"I'd not try it!" said he.

"No?"

"No, sir!"

The moon and the ominous bank of black cloud were very close. There was snow in the air. A thickening flurry ran past.

Uncle Joe West was not on the lookout when Doctor Luke opened the kitchen door at Ragged Run Cove, and strode in, with Billy Topsail at his heels, and with the air of a man who had survived difficulties and was proud of it. Uncle Joe West was sitting by the fire, his face in his hands; and the mother of Dolly West—with Dolly still restlessly asleep in her arms—was rocking, rocking, as before. And Doctor Luke set to work without delay or explanation—in a way so gentle, with a voice so persuasive, with a hand so tender and sure, with a skill and wisdom so keen, that little Dolly West, who was brave enough, in any case, as you know, yielded the additional patience and courage that the simple means at hand for her relief required. Doctor Luke laved Dolly West's blue eyes until she could see again, and sewed up her wounds, that night, so that no scar remained, and in the broad light of the next day picked out grains of powder until not a single grain was left to disfigure the child.

CHAPTER XX

In Which Skinflint Sam of Ragged Run Finds Himself in a Desperate Predicament and Bad-Weather Tom West at Last Has What Skinflint Sam Wants

WELL, now, when all this had been accomplished, and when Dolly had gone to bed with her mother, it occurred to Doctor Luke that he had not clapped eyes on Dolly's father, Bad-Weather Tom West.

"Where's Tom?" said he.

Joe started.

"Wh-wh-where's Tom?" he stammered.

"Ay."

"Have you not heard about Tom?"

Doctor Luke was puzzled.

"No," said he; "not a word."

Joe commanded himself for the tale he had to tell.

"Skipper Tom West," Joe began, "made a wonderful adventure of life in the end. I doubt if ever a man done such a queer thing afore.

'Twas queer enough, sir, I'll be bound, an' you'll say so when I tells you; but 'twas a brave, kind thing, too, though it come perilous close t' the line o' foul play—but that's how you looks at it. Bad-Weather Tom," he went on, "come back from seein' you, sir, in a silent mood. An' no wonder! You told un, sir—well, you told un what you told un, about what he was to expect in this life; an' the news lay hard on his mood. He told nobody here what that news was; nor could the gossips gain a word from his wife.

"'What's the matter with Bad-Weather Tom?' says they.

"'Ask Tom,' says she.

"An' they asked Tom.

"'Tom,' says they, 'what's gone along o' you, anyhow?'

"'Well,' says Tom, 'I found out something I never knowed afore. That's all that's the matter with me.'

"'Did Doctor Luke tell you?'

"'When I talks with Doctor Luke,' says Tom, 'I *always* finds out something I never knowed afore.'

"Whatever you told un, sir—an' I knows what you told un—it made a changed man o' Bad-

Weather Tom. He mooned a deal, an' he would talk no more o' the future, but dwelt upon the shortness of a man's days an' the quantity of his sin, an' laboured like mad, an' read the Scriptures by candle-light, an' sot more store by going to church and prayer-meetin' than ever afore. Labour? Ecod, how that poor man laboured—after you told un. While there was light! An' until he fair dropped in his tracks o' sheer weariness!

"'Twas back in the forest—haulin' fire-wood with the dogs an' storin' it away back o' this little cottage under Lend-a-Hand Hill.

"'Dear man!' says Skinflint Sam; 'you've fire-wood for half a dozen winters.'

"'They'll need it,' says Tom.

"'Ay,' says Sam; 'but will you lie idle next winter?'

"'Nex' winter?' says Tom. An' he laughed. 'Oh, nex' winter,' says he, 'I'll have another occupation.'

"'Movin' away, Tom?'

"'Well,' says Tom, 'I is an' I isn't.'

"There come a day not long ago when seals was thick on the floe off Ragged Run. You mind the time, sir?" Billy Topsail "minded" the time well enough. And so did Doctor Luke. It was the time when Billy Topsail and Teddy Brisk were carried to sea with the dogs on the ice. "Well, you could see the seals with the naked eye from Lack-a-Day Head. A hundred thousand black specks swarmin' over the ice three miles an' more to sea. Ragged Run went mad for slaughter—jus' as it did yesterday, sir. 'Twas a fair time for offshore sealin', too: a blue, still day, with the look an' feel o' settled weather.

"The ice had come in from the current with a northeasterly gale, a wonderful mixture o' Arctic bergs and Labrador pans, all blindin' white in the spring sun; an' 'twas a field so vast, an' jammed so tight against the coast, that there wasn't much more than a lane or two an' a Dutchman's breeches of open water within sight from the heads. Nobody looked for a gale o' offshore wind t' blow that ice t' sea afore dawn o' the next day.

"'A fine, soft time, lads!' says Skinflint Sam. 'I 'low I'll go out with the Ragged Run crew.'

"'Skipper Sam,' says Bad-Weather Tom, 'you're too old a man t' be on the ice.'

"'Ay,' says Sam; "but I wants t' bludgeon another swile afore I dies.'

"'But you *creaks*, man!'

"'Ah, well,' says Sam; 'I'll show the lads I'm able t' haul a swile ashore.'

"'Small hope for such as you on a movin' floe!'

"'Last time, Tom,' says Sam.

"'Last time, true enough,' says Tom, 'if that ice starts t' sea with a breeze o' wind behind!'

"'Oh, well, Tom,' says Sam, 'I'll creak along out an' take my chances. If the wind comes up I'll be as spry as I'm able.'

"It come on to blow in the afternoon. But 'twas short warnin' o' offshore weather. A puff o' gray wind come down. a saucier gust went by; an' then a swirl o' galeish wind jumped off the heads an' come scurrying over the pans. At the first sign o' wind, Skinflint Sam took for home, lopin' over the ice as fast as his lungs an' old legs would take un when pushed, an' nobody worried about *he* any more. He was in such mad haste that the lads laughed behind un as he passed.

"Most o' the Ragged Run crew followed, draggin' their swiles; an' them that started early come safe t' harbour with the fat. But there's nothin' will master a man's caution like the lust o' slaughter. Give a Newfoundlander a club, an' show un a swile-pack, an' he'll venture far from safety. 'Twas not until a flurry o' snow come along of a sudden that the last o' the crew dropped what they was at an' begun t' jump for shore like a pack o' jack-rabbits.

"With snow in the wind 'twas every man for himself. An' that means no mercy an' less help.

"By this time the ice had begun t' feel the wind. 'Twas restless. An' a bad promise. The pans crunched an' creaked as they settled more at ease. The ice was goin' abroad. As the farther fields drifted off t' sea, the floe fell loose inshore. Lanes an' pools opened up. The cake-ice tipped an' went awash under the weight of a man. Rough goin', ecod! There was no tellin' when open water would cut a man off where he stood.

"An' the wind was whippin' offshore, an' the snow was like dust in a man's eyes an' mouth, an' the landmarks o' Ragged Run was nothin' but shadows in a mist o' snow t' windward.

"Nobody knowed where Skinflint Sam was. Nobody thought about Sam. An' wherever poor old Skinflint was—whether safe ashore or creakin' shoreward against the wind on his last legs—he must do for himself. 'Twas no time t' succour rich or poor. Every man for himself an' the devil take the hindmost!

"Bound out, in the mornin', Bad-Weather Tom had fetched his rodney through the lanes. By luck an' good conduct he had managed t' get the wee boat a fairish way out. He had beached her there on the floe—a big pan, close by a hummock which he marked with care. And 'twas for Tom West's little rodney that the seven last men o' Ragged Run was jumpin'. With her afloat—an' the pack loosenin' inshore under the wind—they could make harbour well enough afore the gale worked up the water in the lee o' the Ragged Run hills.

"But she was a mean, small boat. There was room for six, with safety—but room for no more. There was no room for seven. 'Twas a nasty mess, t' be sure. You couldn't expect nothin' else. But there wasn't no panic. Ragged Run men is accustomed t' tight places. An' they took this one easy. Them that got there first launched the boat an' stepped in. No fight: no fuss.

"It just happened t' be Eleazer Butt that was left. 'Twas Eleazer's ill-luck. An' Eleazer was up in years an' had fell behind comin' over the ice.

"'No room for me?' says he.

"'Twas sure death t' be left on the ice. The wind begun t' taste o' frost. An' 'twas jumpin' up. 'Twould carry the floe far an' scatter it broadcast.

"'See for yourself, lad,' says Tom.

"'Pshaw!' says Eleazer. 'That's too bad!'

"'You isn't no sorrier than me, b'y.'

"Eleazer tweaked his beard. 'Dang it!' says he. 'I wisht there *was* room. I'm hungry for my supper.'

"'Let un in,' says one of the lads. ''Tis even chances she'll float it out.'

"'Well,' says Eleazer, 'I doesn't want t' make no trouble ——'

"'Come aboard,' says Tom. 'An' make haste.'

"'If she makes bad weather,' says Eleazer, 'I'll get out.'

"We pushed off from the pan. 'Twas fallin' dusk by this time. The wind blowed black. The frost begun t' bite. Snow come thick—just as if, ecod, somebody up aloft was shakin' the clouds, like bags, in the gale! An' the rodney was deep an' ticklish.

"Had the ice not kep' the water flat in the

lanes an' pools, either Eleazer would have had to get out, as he promised, or she would have swamped like a cup. As it was, handled like dynamite, she done well enough; an' she might have made harbour within the hour had she not been hailed by Skinflint Sam from a small pan o' ice midway between."

Doctor Luke and Billy Topsail were intent on the tale.

"Go on," said Doctor Luke.

"A queer finish, sir."

"What happened?"

CHAPTER XXI

In Which a Crœsus of Ragged Run Drives a Hard Bargain in a Gale of Wind

"AN' there the ol' codger was squattin'," Skipper Joe's tale went on, "his ol' face pinched an' woebegone, his bag o' bones wrapped up in his coonskin coat, his pan near flush with the sea, with little black waves already beginnin' t' wash over it.

"A sad sight, believe me! Poor old Skinflint Sam bound out t' sea without hope on a wee pan o' ice!

"'Got any room for me?' says he.

"We ranged alongside.

"'She's too deep as it is,' says Tom. 'I'm wonderful sorry, Skipper Sam.'

"An' he was.

"'Ay,' says Sam; 'you isn't got room for no more. She'd sink if I put foot in her.'

"'Us'll come back,' says Tom.

"'No use, Tom,' says Sam. 'You knows that well enough. 'Tis no place out here for a Ragged Run punt. Afore you could get t' shore an' back night will be down an' this here gale will be a blizzard. You'd never be able t' find me.'

"'I 'low not,' says Tom.

"'Oh, no,' says Sam. 'No use, b'y.'

"'Skipper Sam,' says Tom, 'I'm sorry!'

"'Ay,' says Sam; ''tis a sad death for an ol' man—squattin' out here all alone on the ice an' shiverin' with the cold until he shakes his poor damned soul out.'

"'Not damned!' cries Tom. 'Oh, don't say it!'

"'Ah, well!' says Sam; 'sittin' here all alone I been thinkin'.'

"''Tisn't by any man's wish that you're here, poor man!' says Tom.

"'Oh, no,' says Sam. 'No blame t' nobody. My time's come. That's all. But I wisht I had a seat in your rodney, Tom.'

"An' then Tom chuckled.

"'What you laughin' at?' says Sam.

"'I got a comical idea,' says Tom.

"'Laughin' at me, Tom?'

"'Oh, I'm jus' laughin'.'

"''Tis neither time nor place, Tom,' says Sam, 't' laugh at an old man.'

"Tom roared. Ay, he slapped his knee, an' he throwed back his head, an' he roared! 'Twas enough almost t' swamp the boat.

"'For shame!' says Sam.

"An' more than Skinflint Sam thought so.

"'Skipper Sam,' says Tom, 'you're rich, isn't you?'

"'I got money,' says Sam.

"'Sittin' out here all alone,' says Tom, 'you been thinkin' a deal, you says?'

"'Well,' says Sam, 'I'll not deny that I been havin' a little spurt o' sober thought.'

"'You been thinkin' that money wasn't much, after all?'

"'Ay.'

"'An' that all your money in a lump wouldn't buy you passage ashore?'

"'Oh, some few small thoughts on that order,' says Sam. ''Tis perfectly natural.'

"'Money talks,' says Tom.

"'Tauntin' me again, Tom?'

"'No, I isn't,' says Tom. 'I means it. Money talks. What'll you give for my seat in the boat?'

"''Tis not for sale, Tom.'

"The lads begun t' grumble. It seemed just

as if Bad-Weather Tom West was makin' game of an ol' man in trouble. 'Twas either that or lunacy. An' there was no time for nonsense off the Ragged Run coast in a spring gale of wind. But I knowed what Tom West was about. You sees, sir, I knowed what you told him. An' as for me, fond as I was o' poor Tom West, I had no mind t' interrupt his bargain.

"'Hist!' Tom whispered t' the men in the rodney. 'I knows what I'm doin'.'

"'A mad thing, Tom!'

"'Oh, no!' says Tom. ''Tis the cleverest thing ever I thought of. Well,' says he to Sam, 'how much?'

"'No man sells his life.'

"'Life or no life, my place in this boat is for sale,' says Tom. 'Money talks. Come, now. Speak up. Us can't linger here with night comin' down.'

"'What's the price, Tom?'

"'How much you got, Sam?'

"'Ah, well, I can afford a stiffish price, Tom. Anything you say in reason will suit me. You name the price, Tom. I'll pay.'

"'Ay, ye crab!' says Tom. 'I'm namin' prices, now. Look you, Sam! You're seventy-three. I'm fifty-three. Will you grant that I'd live t' be as old as you?'

"'I'll grant it, Tom.'

"'I'm not sayin' I would,' says Tom. 'You mark that.'

"'Ah, well, I'll grant it, anyhow.'

"'I been an industrious man all my life, Skipper Sam. None knows it better than you. Will you grant that I'd earn a hundred and fifty dollars a year if I lived?'

"'Ay, Tom.'

"Down come a gust o' wind.

"'Have done!' says one of the lads. 'Here's the gale come down with the dark. Us'll all be cast away.'

"'Rodney's mine, isn't she?' says Tom.

"Well, she was. Nobody could say nothin' t' that. An' nobody did.

"'That's three thousand dollars, Sam,' says Tom. 'Three—thousand—dollars!'

"'Ay,' says Sam, 'she calculates that way. But you've forgot t' deduct your livin' from the total. Not that I minds,' says he. ''Tis just a business detail.'

"'I'll not be harsh!' says Tom.

"'Another thing, Tom,' says Sam. 'You're

askin' me t' pay for twenty years o' life when I can use but a few. God knows how many!'

"'I got you where I wants you,' says Tom, 'but I isn't got the heart t' grind you. Will you pay two thousand dollars for my seat in the boat?'

"'If you is fool enough t' take it, Tom.'

"'There's something t' boot,' says Tom. 'I wants t' die out o' debt.'

"'You does, Tom.'

"'An' my father's bill is squared?'

"'Ay.'

"''Tis a bargain!' says Tom. 'God witness!'

"'Lads,' says Skinflint Sam t' the others in the rodney, 'I calls you t' witness that I didn't ask Tom West for his seat in the boat. I isn't no coward. I've asked no man t' give up his life for me. This here bargain is a straight business deal. Business is business. 'Tis not my proposition. An' I calls you t' witness that I'm willin' t' pay what he asks. He've something for sale. I wants it. I've the money t' buy it. The price is his. I'll pay it.'

"Then he turned to Tom.

"'You wants this money paid t' your wife, Tom?' says he.

"'Ay,' says Tom, 't' my wife. She'll know why.'

"'Very good,' says Skinflint. 'You've my word that I'll do it.' An' then: 'Wind's jumpin' up, Tom.'

"'I wants your oath. The wind will bide for that. Hold up your right hand.'

"Skinflint shivered in a blast o' the gale.

"'I swears,' says he.

"'Lads,' says Tom, 'you'll shame this man to his grave if he fails t' pay!'

"'Gettin' dark, Tom,' says Sam.

"'Ay,' says Tom; ''tis growin' wonderful cold an' dark out here. I knows it well. Put me ashore on the ice, lads,' says he.

"We landed Tom, then, on a near-by pan. He would have it so.

"'Leave me have my way!' says he. 'I've done a good stroke o' business.'

"Presently we took ol' Skinflint aboard in Tom's stead; an' jus' for a minute we hung off Tom's pan t' say good-bye.

"'I sends my love t' the wife an' the children,' says he. 'You'll not fail t' remember. She'll know why I done this thing. Tell her 'twas a grand chance an' I took it.'

"'Ay, Tom.'

"'Fetch in here close,' says Tom. 'I wants t' talk t' the ol' skinflint you got aboard there. I'll have my say, ecod, at last! Ye crab!' says he, shakin' his fist in Skinflint's face when the rodney got alongside. 'Ye robber! Ye pinch-a-penny! Ye liar! Ye thief! I *done* ye! Hear me? I done ye! I vowed I'd even scores with ye afore I died. An' I've done it—I've done it! What did ye buy? Twenty years o' my life! What will ye pay for? Twenty years o' my life!'

"An' Tom laughed. An' then he cut a caper, an' come close t' the edge o' the pan, an' shook his fist in Skinflint's face again.

"'Know what I found out from Doctor Luke?' says he. 'I seen Doctor Luke, ye crab! Know what he told me? No, ye don't! Twenty years o' my life this here ol' skinflint will pay for!' he crowed. 'Two thousand dollars he'll put in the hands o' my poor wife!'

"Well, well! The rodney was movin' away. An' a swirl o' snow shrouded poor Tom West. But we heard un laugh once more.

"'My heart has give 'way!' he yelled. '*I didn't have three months t' live! An' Doctor Luke tol' me so!*'

"Well, now, sir," Skipper Joe concluded, "Skinflint done what he said he would do. He laid the money in the hands o' Tom West's wife last week. But a queer thing happened next day. Up went the price o' pork at Skinflint's shop! And up went the price o' tea an' molasses! An' up went the price o' flour!"

CHAPTER XXII

In Which Doctor Luke and Billy Topsail Go North, and at Candlestick Cove, Returning, Doctor Luke Finds Himself Just a Bit Peckish

A RUMOUR came to Our Harbour, by the tongue of a fur-trader, who stopped over night at Doctor Luke's hospital, on his way to the South, that there was sickness in the North—some need or other; the fur-trader was not sure what. Winter still lingered. The mild spell, which had interrupted the journey of Billy Topsail and Teddy Brisk across Schooner Bay, had been a mere taste of spring. Hard weather had followed. Schooner Bay was once more jammed with ice, which had drifted back —jammed and frozen solid; and the way from Our Harbour to Tight Cove was secure. Teddy Brisk was ready to be moved; and this being so, and the lad being homesick for his mother, and the rumour of need in the North coming down —all this being so, Doctor Luke determined all at once to revisit the northern outports for the last time that winter.

"Are you ready for home, Teddy?" said he.

"I is that, sir!"

"Well," Doctor Luke concluded, "there is no reason why you should not be home. I'll harness the dogs to-morrow and take you across Schooner Bay on the komatik."

"Billy Topsail comin', sir?"

"What say, Billy?"

"May I go, sir?"

"You may."

"All the way, sir?"

"All the way!" cried Doctor Luke. "Why, boy, I'm going north to——"

"Please, sir!"

"Well, well! If you've the mind. Come along, boy. I'll be glad to have you."

Teddy Brisk was taken across Schooner Bay and restored to his mother's arms. And Doctor Luke and Billy Topsail drove the dogs north on Doctor Luke's successful round of visits.

It was on the return journey that Doctor Luke and Billy Topsail fell in with the Little Fiddler of Amen Island. At Candlestick Cove they were to feed the dogs and put up for the night. It was still treacherous March weather; and the night threatened foul—a flurry of snow falling and the sky overcast with a thickening drab scud. Day was done when Doctor Luke and Billy Topsail crawled out of the timber and scurried down Twist Hill. In the early dusk the lights were already twinkling yellow and warm in the cottages below; and from the crest of the long hill, in the last of the light, Amen Island was visible, an outlying shadow, across Ships' Run.

There were still sixty miles left of Doctor Luke's round—this second winter round from Our Harbour to the lonely huts of Laughter Bight, thirty miles north of Cape Blind, touching all the harbours between, and by way of Thunder Tickle and Candlestick Cove, which lay midway, back to the shaded lamp and radiant open fire of the little surgery at Our Harbour.

As the dogs scurried down Twist Hill, whimpering and snarling, eager to make an end of a hard day, Doctor Luke visioned those wintry miles and reflected upon the propriety of omitting a call at Amen Island.

Doctor Luke and Billy Topsail drew up at Mild Jim Cull's.

"Skipper James," said Doctor Luke, in the kitchen, across the lamp-lit, devastated supper table, an hour later, "what's the health of Amen Island?"

"They're all well, sir—so far as I knows."

"All well? Just my luck! Then I won't——"

"Amanda," Skipper James admonished his wife, in a grieved whisper, "the Doctor is wantin' another cup o' tea."

The good woman was astonished.

"He've had——" she began.

Then she blushed—and grasped the pot in a fluster—and——

"Thank you—no more," the Doctor protested.

"Ah, now, sir——"

"No more. Really, you know! I've quite finished. I—well—I—if you please, Mrs. Cull. Half a cup. No more. Thank you."

"An' Billy Topsail, too," said Skipper James.

Billy was abashed.

"No—really!" he began. "I—well—thank you—half a cup!"

"All fit an' well, sir, as I says," Skipper James repeated, relieved, now resuming his conversation with Ductor Luke—"so far as I knows."

"Anybody come across Ships' Run lately?"

"Well, no, sir—nobody but ol' Jack Hulk. Another slice o' pork, Doctor?"

The youngest little Cull tittered, astounded:

"He've had ——"

Amanda covered the youngest little Cull's lips just in time with a soft hand.

"Thank you—no," the Doctor protested again. "I'm quite finished. Nothing more—really! Well," he yielded—"if you will ——"

"You, too, Billy Topsail?" said Skipper James.

"Nothing more, really!" Billy replied, with a grin. And then: "Well—if you will ——"

"No; nobody but ol' Jack Hulk," said Skipper James to Doctor Luke.

"Jack Hulk, you say? Hm-m. When was that?"

"I don't rightly remember, sir. 'Twas less than a fortnight ago. I'll lay t' that much."

"And all well over there?"

"No report o' sickness, sir. Have another cut o' bread, sir, while you're about it."

The Doctor lifted his hand.

"No—really," said he, positively. "No more. Well—I—if you please. Thank you. I seem to be just a bit peckish to-night."

"A cut o' bread, Billy?" said Skipper James.

Billy lifted his hand.

"Not a bite!" he protested. And he winked. "Ah, well," he yielded, "might as well, I 'low. Really, now, I *is* jus' a bit peckish the night."

"No; no report o' sickness on Amen," Skipper James repeated, resuming his conversation, as before.

"Quite sure about that?"

"Well, sir," Skipper James replied, his gray eyes twinkling, "I asked ol' Jack Hulk, an' he said, 'All well on Amen Island. The Lord's been wonderful easy on us this winter. I'd almost go so far as t' say,' says he, 'that He've been lax. We've had no visitation o' the Lord,' says he, 'since the fall o' the year. We don't deserve this mercy. I'm free t' say that. We isn't been livin' as we should. There's been more frivolity on Amen Island this winter than ever afore in my time. It haven't been noticed so far,' says he. 'That's plain enough. An' so as yet,' says he, 'we're all well on Amen Island.'"

The Doctor grinned.

"What's the ice on Ships' Run?" said he

"'Tis tumbled, sir. The bread's at your elbow, sir."

"Thank you. Dogs?"

"No, sir. Ships' Run's jammed with floe ice. A man would have t' foot it across. You bound over, sir?"

Doctor Luke deliberated.

"I think not," said he, then. "No." This was positive. "If they're all as well as that on Amen Island I'll get away for Our Harbour at noon to-morrow. No; no more—really. I—well—I'm almost wolfish, I declare. Thank you—if you please—just a sma-a-all ——"

Billy Topsail burst out laughing.

"What's this mirth?" cried the Doctor.

"Well, sir," Billy chuckled, "you *is* jus' a *bit* peckish the night, sir!"

There was a burst of laughter. At that moment, however, in a cottage on Amen Island, across Ships' Run, nobody was laughing—least of all the Little Fiddler of Amen Island.

CHAPTER XXIII

In Which, While Doctor Luke and Billy Topsail Rest Unsuspecting at Candlestick Cove, Tom Lute, the Father of the Little Fiddler of Amen Island, Sharpens an Axe in the Wood-Shed, and the Reader is Left to Draw His Own Conclusions Respecting the Sinister Business

IT was the boast of the Little Fiddler of Amen Island that he had lamed many a man and maid. "An' ecod!" said he, his blue eyes alight, his clean little teeth showing in a mischievous grin, his round cheeks flushed with delight in the gift of power; "there's no leg between the Norman Light an' Cape Mugford so sodden it can balk me when I've the wind in my favour!"—meaning to imply, with more truth than modesty, that the alluring invitation of his music was altogether irresistible when he was in the mood to provoke a response.

"Had I the will," said he, "I could draw tears from the figurehead o' the *Roustabout*. An' one o' these days, when I've the mind t' show my power," said he, darkly, "maybe I'll do it, too!"

He was young—he was twelve. Terry Lute

was his name. To be known as the Little Fiddler of Amen Island as far north as the world of that coast sailed was the measure of the celebrity he coveted. And that was a good deal: it is a long way for fame to carry—north to the uttermost fishing-berths of the Labrador. Unquestionably the Little Fiddler of Amen Island was of the proportions of a Master.

It was aboard a trading schooner—a fly-by-night visitor at Amen Island (not Skinflint Sam's trader from Ragged Run)—that the Little Fiddler of Amen Island had first clapped eyes on a fiddle and heard the strains of it. That was long ago—oh, long, long ago! Terry Lute was a mere child, then, as he recalled, in a wistful amusement with those old days, and was accustomed to narrate—seven or thereabouts. An' 'twas the month o' June—sweet weather, ecod! (said he) an' after dark an' the full o' the moon. And Terry had harkened to the strain—some plaintive imaginings of the melancholy clerk in the cabin, perhaps; and he had not been able to bear more—not another wail or sob of it (said he)—but had run full tilt to his mother's knee to tell her first of all the full wonder of the adventure.

'Twas called a fiddle (said he)—'twas played with what they called a bow; an' oh, woman (said he), what music could be made by means of it! And Terry could play it—he had seen the clerk sawin' away—sawin' an' sawin' away; an' he had learned how 'twas done jus' by lookin' —in a mere peep. 'Twas nothin' at all t' do (said he)—not a whit o' bother for a clever lad. Jus' give un a fiddle an' a bow—he'd show un how 'twas done!

"I got t' have one, mama!" he declared. "Oo-sh! I jus' got t'!"

His mother laughed at this fine fervour.

"Mark me!" he stormed. "I'll have one o' they fiddles afore very long. An' I'll have folk fair shakin' their legs off t' the music I makes!"

When old Bob Likely, the mail-man, travelling afoot, southbound from Elegant Tickle to Our Harbour and the lesser harbours of Mad Harry and Thank-the-Lord, a matter of eighty miles—when old Bob Likely, on the night of Doctor Luke's arrival at Candlestick Cove, rounded Come-Along Point of Amen Island and searched the shadows ahead for his entertainment, his lodgings for the night were determined and disclosed.

It was late—a flurry of snow falling and the moon overcast with a thickening drab scud; and old Bob Likely's disheartened expectation on the tumbled ice of Ships' Run, between Point o' Bay of the Harbourless Shore and Amen Island, had consequently discovered the cottages of his destination dark—the windows black, the fires dead, the kitchens frosty and the folk of Amen Island long ago turned in.

Of the thirty cottages of Amen, however, snuggled under thick blankets of snow, all asleep in the gray night, one was wide awake—lighted up as though for some festivity; and for the hospitality of its lamps and smoking chimney old Bob Likely shaped his astonished course.

"'Tis a dance!" he reflected, heartening his step. "I'll shake a foot if I lame myself!"

Approaching Tom Lute's cottage from the harbour ice, old Bob Likely cocked his ear for the thump and shuffle of feet and the lively music of the Little Fiddler of Amen Island. It was the Little Fiddler's way to boast: "They'll sweat the night! Mark me! I'm feelin' fine. They'll shed their jackets! I'll have their boots off!"

And old Bob Likely expected surely to discover the Little Fiddler, perched on the back of a chair, the chair aloft on the kitchen table, mischievously delighting in the abandoned antics of the dancers, the while a castaway sealing crew, jackets shed and boots kicked off, executed a reel with the maids of Amen Island.

But there was no music—no thump or shuffle of feet or lively strain; the house was still—except for a whizz and metallic squeaking in the kitchen shed to which old Bob Likely made his way to lay off the sacred bag of His Majesty's Mail and his own raquets and brush himself clean of snow.

Tom Lute was whirling a grindstone by candle-light in the shed. When Bob Likely lifted the latch and pushed in he was interrupted and startled.

"Who's that?" he demanded.

"'Tis His Majesty's Mail, Tom."

"That you, Bob?" Tom's drawn face lightened with heartiness. "Well, well! Come in. You're welcome. We've need of a lusty man in this house the night. If the thing haves t' be done, Bob, you'll come handy for holdin'. You come across from Candlestick?"

Bob threw off his pack.

"No," said he. "I come over from Point o' Bay."

"Up from Laughter Bight, Bob?"

"All the way."

"Any word o' Doctor Luke down north?"

"Ay; he's down north somewheres."

"Whereabouts, Bob?"

"I heard of un at Trap Harbour."

"Trap Harbour! Was he workin' north, Bob?"

"There was sickness at Huddle Cove."

"At Huddle Cove? My, my! 'Tis below Cape Blind. He'll not be this way in a fortnight. Oh, dear me!"

By this time His Majesty's Mail was stamping his feet and brooming the snow from his sealhide boots. In answer to his violence the kitchen door fell ajar. And Bob Likely cocked his ear. Queer sounds—singular scraps of declaration and pleading—issued to the wood-shed.

There was the tap-tap of a wooden leg. Bob Likely identified the presence and agitated pacing of the maternal grandfather of the Little Fiddler of Amen Island. And there was a whimper and a sob. It was the Little Fiddler.

A woman crooned:

"Hush, dear—ah, hush, now!"

A high-pitched, querulous voice:

"That's what we done when I sailed along o' Small Sam Small aboard the *Royal Bloodhound*." And repeated, the wooden leg tap-tapping meanwhile: "That's what we done aboard the *Royal Bloodhound*. Now, mark me! That's what we done t' Cap'n Small Sam Small."

A young roar, then:

"I'll never have it done t' me!"

And the woman again:

"Ah, hush, dear! Never mind! Ah—hush, now!"

To which there responded a defiant bawl:

"I tells you I won't have it done t' me!"

By all this, to be sure, old Bob Likely, with his ear cocked and his mouth fallen open in amazement, was deeply mystified.

"Look you, Tom!" said he, suspiciously; "what you doin' out here in the frost?"

"Who? Me?" Tom was evasive and downcast.

"Ay."

"Nothin' much."

"'Tis a cold place for that, Tom. An' 'tis a poor lie you're tellin'. 'Tis easy t' see, Tom, that you're busy."

"Ah, well, I got a little job on hand."

"What is your job?"

"This here little job I'm doin' now?"

"Ay."

"Nothin' much."

"What *is* it?"

Tom was reluctant. "I'm puttin' an edge on my axe," he replied.

"What for, Tom?"

Tom hesitated. "Well ——" he drawled. And then, abruptly: "Nothin' much." He was both grieved and agitated.

"But what *for?*"

"I wants it good an' sharp."

"What you want it good an' sharp for?"

"An axe serves best," Tom evaded, "when 'tis sharp."

"Look you, Tom!" said Bob; "you're behavin' in a very queer way, an' I gives you warnin' o' the fac'. What happens? Here I comes quite unexpected on you by candle-light in the shed. Who is I? I'm His Majesty's

Mail. Mark that, Tom! An' what does I find you doin'? Puttin' an edge on an axe. I asks you why you're puttin' an edge on your axe. An' you won't tell. If I didn't know you for a mild man, Tom, I'd fancy you was tired o' your wife."

"Tired o' my wife!" Tom exploded, indignantly. "I isn't goin' t' kill my wife!"

"Who *is* you goin' t' kill?"

"I isn't goin' t' kill nobody."

"Well, *what* you goin' t' kill?"

"I isn't goin' t' kill nothin'."

"Well, then," Bob burst out, "what in thunder is you puttin' an edge on your axe for out here in the frost by candle-light at this time o' night?"

"Who? Me?"

"Ay—you!"

"I got some doctorin' t' do."

Bob lifted his brows. "Hum!" he coughed. "You usually do your doctorin' with an axe?" he inquired.

"No," said Tom, uneasily; "not with an axe."

"What you usually use, Tom?"

"What I usually uses, Bob," Tom replied, "is a decoction an' a spoon."

"Somebody recommend an axe for this complaint?"

"'Tisn't that, Bob.' 'Tis this way. When I haves a job t' do, Bob, I always uses what serves best an' lies handy. That's jus' plain common sense an' cleverness. Well, then, jus' now an axe suits me to a tee. An' so I'm puttin' a good edge on the only axe I got."

"An axe," Bob observed, "will do quick work."

"That's jus' what I thought!" cried Tom, delighted. "Quick an' painless."

"There's jus' one trouble about an axe," Bob went on, dryly, "when used in the practice o' medicine. I never heard it stated—but I fancy 'tis true. What's done with an axe," he concluded, "is hard t' repair."

CHAPTER XXIV

In Which Bob Likely, the Mail-Man, Interrupts Doctor Luke's Departure, in the Nick of Time, with an Astonishing Bit of News, and the Ice of Ships' Run Begins to Move to Sea in a Way to Alarm the Stout Hearted

DOCTOR LUKE, having finished his professional round of the Candlestick cottages in good time, harnessed his dogs, with the help of Billy Topsail, soon after noon next day. Evidently the folk of Amen Island were well. They had been frivolous, no doubt—but had not been caught at it. Amen Island was to be omitted. Doctor Luke was ready for the trail to Poor Luck Harbour on the way south. And he shouted a last good-bye to the folk of Candlestick Cove, who had gathered to wish him Godspeed, and laughed in delighted satisfaction with their affection, and waved his hand, and called to his dogs and cracked his whip; and he would have been gone south from Candlestick Cove on the way to Poor Luck and Our Harbour in another instant had he not caught sight of Bob Likely coming up the harbour ice from the direction of the Arctic floe that was then beginning to drive through Ships' Run under the impulse of a stiffening breeze from the north.

It was old Bob Likely with the mail-bag on his back—there was no doubt about that; the old man's stride and crooked carriage were everywhere familiar—and as he was doubtless from Amen Island, and as he carried the gossip of the coast on the tip of his tongue, of which news of illness and death was not the lest interesting variety, Doctor Luke, alert for intelligence that might serve the ends of his work—Doctor Luke halted his team and waited for old Bob Likely to draw near.

"From Amen, Bob?"

"I is, sir. I'm jus' come across the floe."

"Are they all well?"

"Well, no, sir; they isn't. The Little Fiddler is in mortal trouble. I fears, sir, he's bound Aloft."

"Hut!" the Doctor scoffed. "What's the matter with the Little Fiddler?"

"He've a sore finger, sir."

The Doctor pondered this. He frowned—

perplexed. "What sort of a sore finger?" he inquired, troubled.

"They thinks 'tis mortification, sir."

"Gangrene! What do you think, Bob?"

"It looks like it, sir. I seed a case, sir, when I were off sealin' on the ——"

"Was the finger bruised?"

"No, sir; 'twasn't bruised."

"Was it frost-bitten?"

"No, sir; 'twasn't the frost that done it. I made sure o' that. It come from a small cut, sir."

"A simple infection, probably. Did you see a line of demarcation?"

"Sir?"

"It was discoloured?"

"Oh, ay, sir! 'Twas some queer sort o' colour."

"What colour?"

"Well, sir," said Bob, cautiously, "I wouldn't say as t' that. I'd jus' say 'twas some mortal queer sort o' colour an' be content with my labour."

"Was there a definite line between the discolouration and what seemed to be sound flesh?"

Bob Likely scratched his head in doubt.

"I don't quite mind," said he, "whether there was or not."

"Then there was not," the Doctor declared, relieved. "You would not have failed to note that line. 'Tis not gangrene. The lad's all right. That's good. Everybody else well on Amen Island?"

Bob was troubled.

"They're t' cut that finger off," said he, "jus' as soon as little Terry will yield. Las' night, sir, we wasn't able t' overcome his objection. 'Tis what he calls one of his fiddle fingers, sir, an' he's holdin' out——"

"Cut it off? Absurd! They'll not do that."

"Ay; but they will, sir. 'Tis t' be done the night, sir, with the help o' Sandy Lands an' Black Walt Anderson. They're t' cotch un an' hold un, sir. They'll wait no longer. They're afeared o' losin' little Terry altogether."

"Yes; but surely——"

"If 'twere mortification, sir, wouldn't you cut that finger off?"

"At once."

"With an axe?"

"If I had nothing better."

"An' if the lad was obstinate——"

"If an immediate operation seemed to be advisable, Bob, I would have the lad held."

"Well, sir," said Bob, "they thinks 'tis mortification, sir, an' not knowin' no better——"

"Thank you," said the Doctor. He turned to Mild Jim Cull. "Skipper James," said he, "have Timmie take care of the dogs. I'll cross Ships' Run and lance that finger."

Dusk fell on Amen Island. No doctor had happened across the Run. No saving help—no help of any sort, except the help of Sandy Lands and Black Walt Anderson, to hold the rebellious subject—had come.

At Candlestick Cove Doctor Luke had been delayed. The great news of his fortunate passing had spread inland overnight to the tilts of Rattle River. Before the Doctor could get under way for Amen Island, an old dame of Serpent Bend, who had come helter-skelter through the timber, whipping her team, frantic to be in time to command relief before the Doctor's departure, drove up alone, with four frowsy dogs, and desired the extraction of a tooth; but so fearful and coy was she—notwithstanding that she had suffered the tortures of the damned, as she put it, for three months, having missed the Doctor on his northern course—that the Doctor was kept waiting on her humour an hour or more before she would yield to his scoldings and blandishments.

And no sooner had the old dame of Serpent Bend been rejoiced to receive her recalcitrant tooth in a detached relationship than a lad of Trapper's Lake trudged in to expose a difficulty that turned out to be neither more nor less than a pitiable effect of the lack of nourishment; and when an arrangement had been accomplished to feed the lad well and strong again, a woman of Silver Fox was driven in—a matter that occupied Doctor Luke until the day was near spent and the crossing of Ships' Run was a hazard to be rather gravely debated.

"You'll put it off, sir?" Skipper James advised.

The Doctor surveyed the ice of Ships' Run and the sky beyond Amen Island.

"I wish I might," said he, frankly.

"I would, sir."

"I—I can't very well."

"The floe's started down the Run, sir."

"Yes-s," the Doctor admitted, uneasily; "but you see, Skipper James, I—I ——"

CHAPTER XXV

In Which a Stretch of Slush is to be Crossed and Billy Topsail Takes the Law in His Own Hands

IT was falling dusk and blowing up when Doctor Luke and Billy Topsail, gaffs in hand, left the heads of Candlestick Cove for the ice of Ships' Run ; and a spit of frosty snow—driving in straight lines—was in the gale. Amen Island, lying nearly in the wind's eye, was hardly distinguishable, through the misty interval, from the blue-black sky beyond.

There was more wind in the northeast—more snow and a more penetrating degree of frost. It was already blowing at the pitch of half a gale: it would rise to a gale in the night, thick with snow, it might be, and blowing bitter cold—the wind jumping over the point of Amen Island on a diagonal and sweeping down the Run.

Somewhere to leeward of Candlestick Cove the jam had yielded to the rising pressure of the wind. The floe was outward bound from the

Run. It was already moving in the channel, scraping the rocks of both shores—moving faster as the pans below ran off to open water and removed their restraint.

As yet the pans and hummocks were in reasonably sure contact all the way from Candlestick Cove to Come-Along Point of Amen Island; but the ice was thinning out with accelerating speed—black water disclosing itself in widening gaps—as the compression was relieved. All the while, thus, as Doctor Luke and Billy Topsail made across, the path was diminishing.

In the slant of the wind the ice in the channel of Ships' Run was blown lightly against the Candlestick coast. About the urgent business of its escape to the wide water of Great Yellow Bay the floe rubbed the Candlestick rocks in passing and crushed around the corner of Dead Man's Point.

Near Amen Island, where the wind fell with less force, there was a perilous line of separation. In the lee of the Amen hills—close inshore—the ice was not disturbed: it hugged the coast as before; but outward of this—where the wind dropped down—a lane of water was opening between the inert shore ice and the wind-blown main floe.

As yet the lane was narrow; and there were pans in it—adrift and sluggishly moving away from the Amen shore. When Doctor Luke and Billy Topsail came to this widening breach they were delayed—the course was from pan to pan in a direction determined by the exigency of the moment; and when they had drawn near the coast of Amen—having advanced in a general direction as best they could—they were halted altogether.

And they were not then under Come-Along Point, but on a gathering of heavy Arctic ice, to the north, at the limit of Ships' Run, under that exposed head of Amen, called Deep Water Head, which thrusts itself into the open sea.

"We're stopped, sir," Billy Topsail declared. "We'd best turn back, sir, while there's time."

A way of return was still open. It would be laborious—nothing worse.

"One moment——"

"No chance, sir."

"I'm an agile man, Billy. One moment. I——"

Billy Topsail turned his back to a blast of the

gale and patiently awaited the issue of Doctor Luke's inspection of the path.

"A man can't cross that slush, sir," said he.

Past Deep Water Head the last of the floe was driving. There is a wide little cove there—it is called Deep Water Cove; and there is deep water—a drop of ten fathoms (they say)—under Deep Water Cliff. There was open water in both directions beyond the points of the cove. A detour was thus interrupted.

Doctor Luke and Billy Topsail confronted the only ice that was still in contact with the shore. At no time had the floe extended far beyond Deep Water Head. A high sea, rolling in from the northeast, had played under the ice; and this had gone on for three days—the seas running in and subsiding: all the while casting the ice ponderously against the rocks.

Heavy Arctic ice—fragments of many glacial bergs—had caught the lesser, more brittle drift-pans of the floe against the broken base and submerged face of Deep Water Cliff and ground them slowly to slush in the swells. There were six feet of this slush, perhaps—a depth of six feet and a width of thirty.

It was as coarse as cracked ice in a freezer.

It was a quicksand. Should a man's leg go deep enough he would not be able to withdraw it; and once fairly caught—both feet gripped—he would inevitably drop through. It would be a slow and horrible descent—like sinking in a quicksand.

It was near dark. The snow—falling thicker—was fast narrowing the circle of vision.

"I might get across," said Doctor Luke.

"You'll not try, sir," Billy Topsail declared, positively. "You'll start back t' Candlestick Cove."

"I might ——"

"You'll not!"

There was something in Billy Topsail's tone to make Doctor Luke lift his brows and stare.

"What's that?" said he, smiling grimly.

"I says you'll not try."

Doctor Luke laughed uneasily.

"No?"

"No, sir."

Billy Topsail was a big boy. Doctor Luke measured his length and breadth and power with new interest and recalled that he had always admired the lusty proportions of the lad.

Decidedly—Billy Topsail was a big fellow! And Billy Topsail's intentions were plain.

"Now ——" the Doctor began, argumentatively.

"'Tis no use, sir. I knows you."

Doctor Luke moved off a step. "But Billy, you see, my dear fellow ——"

"No, sir!" Billy Topsail moved within reach.

"I'm quite sure ——"

"No."

Doctor Luke stared at the breach of slush. He faced away, then, abruptly. "Wel-ll," he admitted, with a shrug, "no doubt you're right, Billy. I ——"

CHAPTER XXVI

In Which it Seems that an Axe and Terry Lute's Finger Are Surely to Come into Injurious Contact, and Terry Lute is Caught and Carried Bawling to the Block, While His Mother Holds the Pot of Tar

IN Tom Lute's cottage beyond Come-Along Point of Amen Island they were ready for the operation. There was a thick, round billet of birch, upended in the middle of the kitchen floor, to serve as a block for the amputation; and the axe was sharp, at last—at hand, too, but concealed, for the moment, behind the pantry door—and a pot of tar was warming on the kitchen stove.

Sandy Lands had reported for duty, whom nothing but a sense of duty had drawn to a hand in the surgical assistance—a bit perturbed, as he contemplated the task of restraining the struggles of a violent little subject, whose temper he knew, but sturdy and resolved, his resolution substantiated by a sort of religious austerity.

Black Walt Anderson, a gigantic, phlegmatic fellow, who would have subdivided into half a dozen little Terry Lutes, also awaited the signal to pounce upon the Little Fiddler of Amen Island, imprison his arms, confine his legs, subdue all his little struggles, in short, bear him to the block and flatten his hand and spread his fingers for the severing blow.

It was to be a simple operation—a swift descent of the axe and a quick application of hot tar and bandages to stifle the wound. And that was to be the end of the finger and the trouble.

There had been a good deal of trouble. Terry Lute's sore finger was a source of brutal agony. There had been many days of this pain—a throbbing torture in the finger and hand and arm. And Terry had practiced deception in an heroic degree.

No pain (said he); but, ah, well, a twinge, now an' again—but nothin' at all t' make a man complain. An' sure (said he), 'twas better all the while—improvin' every blessed minute, sir. A day more (said he) would see the boil yield t' mother's poultice; an' a fortnight would see un all healed up an' the finger able for labour again.

It was in the night that Terry could conceal the agony no longer—deep in the night, when his mother sat beside the cot; and then he would crawl out of bed, stow his slender little body away in his mother's arms, put his head down and cry and moan without shame until he had exhausted himself and fallen into a fitful sleep.

No; it was no trifling agony for Terry Lute to withstand. And he knew all the while, moreover, that the cut of an axe—no more, it might be, than a flash—would eventually relieve him. Terry Lute was not afraid of the pain of the thing they wanted to do. That was not the inspiration of his infuriated rebellion.

There was nothing mistaken in the intention of the axe. It was neither cruel nor blundering.

Amen Island lies remote: the folk do for themselves—they are nearly sufficient to themselves, indeed, in all the affairs of life; and when they fail (they say) and sorrow comes of it—well, there is failure everywhere, too, and life leaves every man when the spirit is finished with its habitation. "I done the best I could!" It is epitaph honourable enough. There was no horror on Amen Island—no furious complaint of the wrongs of a social arrangement—when catastrophe came through lack of uncommon means to stave it off.

And so when Tom Lute told old Bob Likely that when he had a job to do he was accustomed to employ the best means at hand—he expressed in simple terms the lesson of his habitat. This affair of Terry Lute's finger was of gravest moment; had the finger gangrened—it must come off in haste, and the sooner the better; and an axe and a pot of tar were the serviceable instruments according to the teaching of all experience.

Doubtless doctors were better provided and more able; but as there was no doctor to be had, and as Terry Lute was loved and greatly desired in the flesh, and as he was apparently in peril of a sudden departure—and as he was in desperate pain—and as ——

But Terry Lute would not have his finger off. From the corner, where he stood at bay, roaring in a way to silence the very gale that had now begun to shake the cottage, he ran to his mother's knee, as though for better harbour.

And there he sobbed his complaint.

"Ah, Terry, lad," his father pleaded; "'tis only a finger!"

"'Tis on my left hand!"

"You're not left-handed, son," Tom Lute

argued, patiently. "You've no real need o' four fingers there. Why, sonny, boy, once I knowed a man ——"

"'Tis one o' my fiddle fingers."

Tom Lute sighed. "Fiddle fingers, son!" said he. "Ah, now, boy! You've said that so often, an' so foolishly, that I ——"

"I'll not have it off!"

"But ——"

"Isn't no *use* in havin' it off," Terry complained, "an' I can't spare it. This here boil ——"

"'Tisn't a boil, son. 'Tis mortification. An' ——"

"'Tis not mortification."

Again Tom sighed.

"Is you afeared, Terry?" said he. "Surely you isn't a pullin' little coward, is you? A finger! 'Tis such a simple little thing t' suffer ——"

"I'm not afeared neither!"

"Well, then ——"

"You may cut any finger you likes off my right hand," Terry boasted, "an' I'll not whimper a peep."

"I don't want a finger off your right hand, Terry."

"I won't have it!"

"'Tis no pleasure t' me t' ——"

"I won't have a finger off my left hand!"

"I tells you, Terry, you isn't left-handed. I've told you that a thousand times. What in the name o' ——"

"I tells you I won't have it!"

Black Walt Anderson looked to Tom Lute for a signal. Sandy Lands rose.

"Now?" he seemed to inquire.

Tom Lute shook his head.

"That's the way we done aboard the *Royal Bloodhound*," the Little Fiddler's grandfather put in. He began to pace the floor. The tap-tap of his wooden leg was furious and his voice was as gusty as the gale outside. "Now, you mark me!" he ran on. "We chopped Cap'n Sam Small's foot off with a axe an' plugged it with b'ilin' tar. 'Twas mortification. I knows mortification when I sees it. An' Sam Small got well."

He was bawling, by this time, like a skipper in a gale—being deaf, the old man was accustomed to raise his voice, a gradual *crescendo*, until he had come as near hearing himself as possible.

"Yes, sir—you mark me! That's what we done aboard the *Royal Bloodhound* the year I shipped for the seals along o' Small Sam Small. We chopped it clean off with a meat axe an' plugged it with b'ilin' tar. If Small Sam Small had clung t' that member for another day he would have died. Mark me! Small Sam Small would have been dropped over the side o' the *Royal Bloodhound* an' left t' shift for hisself in a sack an' a Union Jack!"

He paused before Terry Lute and shook a lean finger under the little boy's nose.

"Now," he roared, "you mark me!"

"I isn't aboard the *Royal Bloodhound!*" Terry sobbed.

"Ah, Terry!" This was Terry's mother. She was crying bitterly. "You'll die an you don't have that finger off!"

"I'll die an I got to!"

"Oh, Terry, Terry!"

"I isn't afeared t' die."

"Ah, Terry, dear, whatever would I do——"

"I'll die afore I gives up one o' my fiddle fingers."

"But you isn't got——"

"Never you mind about that!"

"If you had ——"

"You jus' wait till I grows up!"

Again Sandy Lands inquired for the signal. Tom Lute lifted a hand to forbid.

"Terry, son," said he, gravely, "once an' for all, now, will you ——"

"No!" Terry roared.

"Oh, oh, Terry, dear!" the mother wailed, observing the preparations that were making behind Terry's back. "If you'd only ——"

Terry screamed in a furious passion:

"Have done, woman! I tells you I won't have none o' my fiddle fingers cut off!"

It was the end. Tom Lute gave the signal. Sandy Lands and Black Walt Anderson pounced upon little Terry Lute and carried him bawling and struggling from his mother's knee towards the block of birch in the middle of the kitchen floor. Tom Lute stood waiting there with the axe.

As for Terry Lute's mother, she flew to the stove, tears streaming from her eyes, her mouth grim, and fetched the pot of tar. And then all at once the Little Fiddler of Amen Island wriggled out of the clutches of his captors—they were too tender with him—and dived under the kitchen table.

CHAPTER XXVII

In Which Doctor Luke's Flesh Creeps, Billy Topsail Acts Like a Bob-Cat, and the Little Fiddler of Amen Island Tells a Secret

CONFRONTING the slush of Deep Water Cove, with the finger of the Little Fiddler of Amen Island awaiting his ministration beyond, Doctor Luke had misled the faithful Billy Topsail into the assumption of his acquiescence. It was not in his mind to return to Candlestick Cove that night. It was in his mind to gain the shore and proceed upon his professional call. And there was reason in this. For when the group of Arctic ice—still rhythmically swinging in and out with the great seas from the open—drove down upon the broken base of Deep Water Cliff, it compressed the ice between.

At the moment of greatest compression the slush was reasonably solid ground. When the Arctic ice subsided with the wave, the slush expanded in the wider space it was then permitted to occupy. A man could cross—a light, agile man, daring the depth of the slush, might be able to cross—when the slush was compressed. No man could run all the way across. It must be in two advances. Midway he would be caught by the subsidence of the wave. From this he must preserve himself.

And from this—from dropping through the field of slush and having it close over his head—he might preserve himself by means of his gaff.

"Wel-ll," Doctor Luke had admitted, apparently resigned, "no doubt you're right, Billy. I ——"

Now the Arctic ice was poised.

"Ay, sir. An' you're more reasonable than ever I knowed you t' ——"

A sea was rolling in.

"Wel-ll," the Doctor drawled, "as I grow older ——"

Then came the moment of advantage. Doctor Luke ran out on the slush before Billy Topsail could reach out a hand to restrain him. It was indiscreet. Doctor Luke had been too eager to escape—he had started too soon; the sea was not down—the slush was not squeezed tight. A foot sank to the ankle. Doctor Luke jerked it out. The other foot went down to the calf of the leg. Doctor Luke jerked it—tugged it. It was fast.

The slush, in increasing compression, had caught it. He must wait for the wave to subside.

His flesh crept with the horror of the thing. He was trapped—caught fast! A moment later the sea was in retreat from the cliff and the slush began rapidly to thin. Doctor Luke employed the stratagem that is familiar to the coast for dealing with such ice as the slush in which he was entrapped. He waited—alert. There would come a moment when the consistency of the ice would be so thin that he would drop through.

Precisely before that moment—when his feet were first free—he dropped flat on his gaff. Having in this way distributed his weight—avoided its concentration on a small area—he was borne up. And he withdrew his feet and waited for the sea to fall in again and compress the ice.

When the next wave fell in Billy Topsail started across the ice like a bob-cat

Doctor Luke lay inert through two waves. When the third fell he jumped up and ran towards the base of Deep Water Cliff. Again the sea caught him unaware. His flesh was creeping again. Horror of the stuff underfoot—the treacherous insecurity of it—drove him. The shore was close. He was too eager for the shore—he ran too far; and his foot went down again—foot and leg to the thigh. As instinctively he tried violently to extract the leg by stepping up on the other foot—that leg went down to the knee.

A fall to the arm-pits impended—a drop clean through and overhead. The drop would inevitably be the result of a flash of hesitation. Doctor Luke cried out. And as he cried he plunged forward—a swift, conscious effort to fall prone on his gaff. There was a blank. Nothing seemed to happen. He was amazed to discover that the gaff upheld him. It occurred to him, then, that his feet were trapped—that he could not withdraw his legs from the sucking slush.

Nor could he. They were caught. And he perceived that they were sinking deeper—that he was slowly slipping through the slush.

He was conscious of the night—the dark and snow and wind; and he fancied that he heard a voice of warning.

"Cotch hold ——"

It was a voice.

"Cotch hold o' the gaff!"

Doctor Luke seized the end of Billy Topsail's gaff and drew himself out of the grip of the slush. When the sea came in again he jumped up and joined Billy Topsail on the broken base of Deep Water Cliff. He was breathing hard. He did not look back. Billy Topsail said that they had better make haste—that somebody would "cotch a death o' cold" if they did not make haste. And they made haste.

An hour or more later Doctor Luke, with Billy Topsail in his wake, thrust into Tom Lute's agitated kitchen and interrupted the amputation of the fiddle finger of the Little Fiddler of Amen Island with a "Well, well, well! What in the name of ——" and stood staring—all dusted with snow and shivering and fairly gone purple with cold.

They had Terry Lute cornered, then—his back against the wall, his face horrified, his mouth wide open in a bellow of rage; and Sandy Lands and Black Walt Anderson were almost upon him—and Tom Lute was grimly ready with the axe and Terry Lute's mother was standing beside the round birch block with the pot of tar in her hands and her apron over her head.

Doctor Luke stood staring at all this—his mouth as wide open, because of a temporary paralysis, due to his amazement, as Terry Lute's mouth was fallen in anger and terror. And it was not long after that—the Doctor being warm and dry, then, and the kitchen quiet and expectant, and Tom Lute and Terry Lute's mother exhibiting relief and the keenest sort of interest—that the Doctor took Terry Lute's fiddle finger in his hand.

Then he began to prepare the finger for the healing thrust of a lance.

"I'm going to cure it, Terry," said he.

"That's good, sir. I'm wonderful glad t' save that finger."

"You cherish that finger, Terry?"

"I does that, sir! I've need of it, sir."

The Doctor was not attending. His attention was on the lance and its object. "Mm-m," he ran on, absently, to make distracting conversation. "You've need of it, eh?"

"'Tis one o' my fiddle fingers, sir."

"Mm-m? Ah! The Little Fiddler of Amen Island! Well, Terry, lad, you'll be able to play your fiddle again in a fortnight."

Terry grinned.

"No, sir," said he. "I won't be playin' my fiddle by that time."

The Doctor looked up in astonishment.

"Yes, you will," he flashed, sharply.

"No, sir."

"But I tell you ——"

"I isn't got no fiddle."

"What!"

"All I got now," said the Little Fiddler of Amen Island, "is a jew's-harp. *But jus' you wait till I grows up!*"

Billy Topsail had broken into smothered laughter; and Doctor Luke, laughing, too, had already determined that the Little Fiddler of Amen Island should not have to wait until he grew up for his first violin (which came to pass in due course)—this hearty mirth was in progress when there was a loud knock on the door, a trample of feet in the entry, a draught of cold air blowing through the open door, and Billy Topsail had the surprise of his not uneventful career. He stared, helpless with amazement, incredulity, delight; and for a moment he could do nothing more worthy of his manners than keep on staring, as though he had clapped eyes on a ghost.

Archie Armstrong had come in.

"Archie!" Doctor Luke exclaimed.

They shook hands. But Archie Armstrong's eyes were not on Doctor Luke. Doctor Luke might be met anywhere at any time. It was not surprising to find him on Amen Island. Archie was staring at Billy Topsail.

"Ye little lobster!" said he, at last, grinning.

"Whoop!" Billy yelled. "'Tis you!"

They flew at each other. It was like a wrestling bout. Each in the bear-like embrace of the other, they staggered over the floor and eventually fell down exhausted. And then they got up and shook hands in what Archie called "the regular" way.

CHAPTER XXVIII

In Which Sir Archibald Armstrong's Son and Heir is Presented for the Reader's Inspection, Highly Complimented and Recommended by the Author, and the Thrilling Adventure, Which Archie and Billy are Presently to Begin, Has its Inception on the Departure of Archie From St. John's Aboard the "Rough and Tumble"

AS everybody in St. John's knew very well (and a good many folk of the outports, to say nothing of a large proportion of the sealing fleet), Archie Armstrong was the son of Sir Archibald Armstrong, who was used to calling himself a fish-dealer, but was, in fact, a deal more than that. Directly or indirectly, Sir Archibald's business interests touched every port in Newfoundland, every cove of the Labrador, the markets of Spain and Portugal, of the West Indies and the South American Republics.

His fishing schooners went south to the Banks and north to the gray, cold seas off Cape Chidley; his whalers gave chase in the waters of the Gulf and the Straits; his trading schooners ran from port to port of all that rugged coast; his barques carried cod and salmon and oil to all the markets of the world. And when the ice came down from the north in the spring of the year, his sealing vessels sailed from St. John's on the great adventure.

Archie was Sir Archibald's son. There was no doubt about that. He was a fine, hearty lad —robust, as every young Newfoundlander should be; straight, agile, alert, with head carried high; merry, quick-minded, ready-tongued, fearless in wind and high sea, as a good many adventures with Billy Topsail had proved. His hair was tawny, his eyes as blue as Billy Topsail's, and as wide and as clear; and his face was broad and good-humoured.

And (every lad has his amiable weakness) Archie was something of a dandy in his dress— a tailored, speckless, polished, fashionable person, to whom the set of his trousers and the knot in his cravat were matters of concern. All in all, from his soles to his crown, and from his rosy skin to the innermost recesses of his good red heart, he was very much of a brave, kindly, self-respecting man.

Billy Topsail liked him. That is putting it mildly. And Archie Armstrong liked Billy Topsail. That, too, is putting it mildly. The boys had been through some hard places together, as I have elsewhere recorded; and they had come through the good and the bad of their undertakings with mutual respect and liking. Nobody could help liking Billy Topsail—he was a courageous, decent, jolly, friendly soul; and for the same reasons nobody could help liking Archie Armstrong. It was a good partnership—this friendship between the Colonial knight's son and heir and the outport fisherman's lad. And both had profited.

Billy had gained in manners and knowledge of the world, to describe the least gain that he won; and Archie had gained in health and courage and the wisdom of the coast. But that was all. Rich as Archie's prospects were, and as great the wealth and generosity of his father, Billy Topsail had never anticipated a material advantage; and had one been offered him, it would not have been accepted except on terms of a description not to wound Billy Topsail's self-respect.

Well, what sort of an education had Archie Armstrong had? It is best described in the incident that sent him off on his first sealing voyage, as elsewhere set down. It was twilight of a blustering February day. Sir Archibald Armstrong sat alone in his office, with his chair drawn close to the low, broad window, which overlooked the wharves and ice-strewn harbour beyond; and while the fire roared and the wind drove the snow against the panes, he lost himself in profound meditation.

He stared absently at the swarm of busy men —now almost hidden in the dusk and storm— and at the lights of the sealing fleet, which lay there fitting out for the voyage to the drift-ice of the north; but no sound of the activity on dock or deck could disturb the quiet of the little office where the fire blazed and crackled and the snow fell softly against the window panes.

By and by Archie came in.

"Come, son," said Sir Archibald, presently, "let us watch them fitting out the fleet."

They walked to the window, Sir Archibald with his arm over Archie's shoulder; and in the dusk outside, the wharves and warehouses and ships told the story of the wealth of Sir Archibald's firm.

"It will all be yours some day," said Sir Archibald, gravely. After a pause, he continued: "The firm has had an honourable career through three generations of our family. My father gave it to me with a spotless reputation. More than that, with the business he gave me the faith of every man, woman and child of the outports. The firm has dealt with its fishermen and sealers as man with man, not as the exploiter with the exploited. It has never wronged, or oppressed, or despised them.

"In September you are going to an English public school, and thence to an English University, when the time comes. You will meet with new ideals. The warehouses and ships, the fish and fat, will not mean so much to you. You will forget. It may be even—for you are something of a dandy, you know—that you will be ashamed to acknowledge that your father is a dealer in fish and seal-oil; and that ——"

Archie drew breath to protest.

"But I want you to remember," Sir Archibald went on, lifting his hand. "I want you to know a man when you meet one, whatever the clothes he wears. The men upon whom the fortunes of this firm are founded are true men. They are strong, brave and true. Their work is toilsome and perilous, and their lives are not unused to deprivation; but they are cheerful, and independent, and fearless, through it all—stout hearts, every one of them.

"They deserve respectful and generous treatment at the hands of their employers. For that reason I want you to know them more intimately—to know them as shipmates know one another—that you may be in sympathy with them. I am confident that you will respect them, because I know that you love all manly qualities. And so for your good, and the good of the men, and the good of the firm, I have decided that ——"

"That I may go sealing?" cried Archie.

"That you may go sealing."

Archie had gone sealing. And the adventure had made of him the man that he was.

Archie Armstrong had gone then to an English public school, having made the acquaintance of Billy Topsail on that first voyage, where the friendship had been founded in peril and a narrow escape. And he had come back unspoiled; and he had adventured with Billy Topsail again, and he had gone to England and returned to Newfoundland once more. In St. John's, with an English tutor, because of the illness of his mother, who had by that time recovered, he pleaded with Sir Archibald to be permitted once more to sail with the fleet.

There was objection. Archie was importunate. Sir Archibald relented and gave a reluctant consent. And it was determined that Archie should be shipped with Cap'n Saul Galt, commanding the *Rough and Tumble*, a stout ship, well manned, and, in the hands of Cap'n Saul, as safe a berth for a lad as any ship of the fleet could provide. That Archie was delighted goes without saying; and that he was all aflame with interest in the movements of the ice—inquisitive and talkative—goes without saying too.

As a matter of fact, a man might hear what he liked on the water-front about the movements of the ice. In the gathering places it was just the same. There were rumours of the ice all the way from the Straits of Belle Isle and the Labrador coast to the Funks and Cape Bonavist'. It was even held by some old sealing dogs that the floes had gone to the east in a spurt of westerly weather and would be found far to sea in the southerly drift.

All this while old Cap'n Saul, of the *Rough and Tumble*, with Archie usually at his elbow, cocked an ear and kept his counsel, putting two and two together, and arriving at the correct result of four, according to the old cock's habit.

"The ice is inside the Funks, Archie," said he. 'I'll twist the *Rough and Tumble* t' the west an' shake off the fleet in the night. Havin' clung with profit t' my sealin' wisdom these ten sealin' seasons," he went on, "they'll follow me an they're able, an' pester my fellows an' steal my panned fat. They're all bit mad by the notion that the ice drove t' the east with the nor'west puff an' whisper o' wind we had. I'll fiddle their wits this year—mark me!"

"*Whisper* of wind?" Archie exclaimed. "'Twas a whole *gale* of wind!"

"Pt!"

"And the ice *did* drive to the east."

"Pt!" says Cap'n Saul. "You'll never make a sealin' skipper, Archie. I smells the ice off the Horse Islands."

It was foul weather all the way from St. John's to the floes. The fleet sailed into a saucy head-wind and a great slosh of easterly sea. It was a fair start and no favour, all managed by the law; the fat on the floes was for the first crews of the fleet to find and slaughter it. And there was a mighty crowd on the water-front to wish the fleet well; and there was a vast commotion, too—cheering and waving and the popping of guns.

At sea it was a helter-skelter race for the ice. Cap'n Saul touched up the *Rough and Tumble* beyond St. John's Narrows; and the ship settled to her work, in that rough and tumble of black water, with a big white bone in her teeth—shook her head and slapped her tail and snouted her way along to the northeast. A whisp of fog came with the night. It was thick weather. But Cap'n Saul drove northeast, as before—slap into a smothering sea; and by this the fleet, tagging behind, was befooled and misled.

After dark, Cap'n Saul doused the lights and switched full steam to the west; and when day broke the *Rough and Tumble* was alone, come what might of her isolation—and come it did, in due course, being all a-brew for Cap'n Saul and crew, even then, in the northwest.

As for the fleet, it was off on fools' business in the bare seas to the east.

CHAPTER XXIX

In Which the Crew of the "Rough and Tumble" is Harshly Punished, and Archie Armstrong, Having Pulled the Wool Over the Eyes of Cap'n Saul, Goes Over the Side to the Floe, Where He Falls in with a Timid Lad, in Whose Company, with Billy Topsail Along, He is Some Day to Encounter His Most Perilous Adventure

WELL, now, two days later, near dusk, with Archie Armstrong on the bridge, the *Rough and Tumble* was crawling northwest through the first ice of the floe. An hour of drab light was left of the day—no more. And it was mean ice roundabout—small pans and a naughty mess of slush. There was a hummock or two, it might be, and a clumper or two, as well; and a man might travel that ice well enough, sore pinched by need to do so. But it was foul footing for the weight of a full-grown man, and tricky for the feet of a lad; and a man must dance a crooked course, and caper along, or perish—leap from a block that would tip and sink under his feet to a pan that would bear him up until he had time and the wit to leap again, and so come, at last, by luck and good conduct, to a pan stout enough for pause.

It was mean ice, to be sure. Yet there was a fine sign of seals drifting by. Here and there was an old dog hood on a hummock; and there and here were a harp and a whitecoat on a flat pan. But the orders of Cap'n Saul were to "leave the swiles be"—to "keep the mouths o' the guns shut" until the *Rough and Tumble* had run up to the herd that was coming down with the floe.

"I'll have no swiles slaughtered in play," he declared.

A gun popped forward. It was from the midst of a crowd. And Cap'n Saul leaned over the bridge-rail.

"Who done that?" he demanded.

There was no answer.

"Mm-m?" Cap'n Saul repeated. "Who done that?"

No answer.

"A dog hood lyin' dead off the port bow!" said Cap'n Saul. "Who killed un?"

Still no answer. And Cap'n Saul didn't ask again. Forthwith he stopped the ship.

"Mister Knibbs, sir," said he, to the mate, "send the crew after that dead hood."

The mate jumped.

"Cap'n Saul, sir," he replied, his eyes popping, "the ice ——"

"Sir?"

"This here ice, sir——"

"*Sir?*"

"This here——"

"SIR?"

"This ——"

"Mister Knibbs, sir," said Cap'n Saul, dryly, "this here ice is fit enough for any crew that I commands. An' if the crew isn't fit for the ice, sir, I'll soon have un so, ecod! Put un over the side. We'll waste no swiles on this v'y'ge."

"All hands, sir?"

"All hands over the side, sir, t' fetch that dead hood aboard."

Archie put in:

"May I go, Cap'n Saul?"

"No!"

"Cap'n Saul," Archie began to wheedle, "I'm so wanting to——"

"No, sir."

"I'm just crazy to——"

"'Tis no fit place for you."

"But——"

Cap'n Saul changed his mind all at once. He sent a call for Archie's old and well-tried friend, Bill o' Burnt Bay.

"Stand by the lad," said he.

"Ay, sir."

Archie left the bridge with Bill o' Burnt Bay, with whom he had sailed before. And over the side they went. And over the side went the crew for punishment. There were more than two hundred men. And not a man was spared. Cap'n Saul sent the ship's doctor after malingerers, and the mate and the haft of a sealing gaff after lurkers; and he kept them capering and balancing for dear life on that dirty floe, sopping and shivering, all in a perilous way, until dusk was in the way of catching some of them unaware.

It was then that Archie and Bill o' Burnt Bay fell in with old Jonathan Farr of Jolly Harbour. Bill o' Burnt Bay knew the old man well. And he was shocked to find him cavorting over that foul, tricky ice, with the thin blood and dry old bones he had to serve his need—a gray old dog like Jonathan Farr of Jolly Harbour, past his full labour these years gone by, gone stiff and all unfit for the labour and chances of the ice.

Still, the old man was blithe enough, as Bill marvelled to see. His eye was lit up with a flicker of fun, sparkling, somehow, through the rheum of age; and his words were mixed with laughter. They came to rest on a pan—the four of them together; old Jonathan Farr and Bill and Archie and a little lad. And Archie marked this in a glance—that the lad, whoever he was, was out of heart with the work he was at.

A good deal was to flow from that meeting; and Billy Topsail was to have a part in it all.

CHAPTER XXX

In Which a Little Song-Maker of Jolly Harbour Enlists the Affection of the Reader

"MY gran'son, Bill," said Jonathan.

Archie pitied the lad—a white, soft-eyed little chap, all taut and woeful with anxiety.

"He's young for the ice," Bill observed.

"A young dog," Jonathan replied, "masters his tricks with ease."

Again Archie pitied the little fellow.

"Too young," said Bill, "for man's labour like this."

"He'll l'arn all the better for his youth."

"Time enough," Bill insisted, "two years hence."

"Ah, well, Bill," said Jonathan, then, "I wants t' see my gran'son fit an' able for his labour afore I goes my way." And he clapped the lad on the back. "Eh, Toby?" said he, heartily.

The lad was grave and mannerly.

"Ay, gran'pa," said he; "you're wonderful careful o' me, you is!"

"That I is, Toby!"

"Yes, siree!"

"I bet I is careful o' you!" Jonathan declared. "An' I'll keep on bein' so. Eh, Toby?"

The lad turned to Archie.

"I'm havin' a wonderful bringin' up, sir," said he. "My gran'pa is wonderful careful o' me. With the wonderful bringin' up I'm havin' I ought t' turn out a wonderful clever man."

"You will!" Archie replied.

"That ye will!" said Bill o' Burnt Bay.

"Pray God," said the lad, "I'm worthy!"

Jonathan gave the lad a little clap on the back. Archie thought it was to thank him for the expression of confidence. And it made the lad squirm and grin like a patted puppie.

"What you think of un, Bill?" Jonathan inquired.

It was a wistful question. Jonathan seemed to want a word of praise. And Bill gave it with all his heart.

"Big as a whale!" said he.

"He've the hull of a young whale," said Jonathan; "an' afore this v'y'ge is out he'll have the heart of a bear."

Toby chuckled.

"Ay—maybe!" said he.

"You will!" Archie declared.

Well, now, you must know that it is not uncommon to fall in with a timid lad on the coast: a lad given a great deal to music and the making of ballads, and to the telling of tales, too. Such folk are timid when young. It is no shame. By and by they harden to their labour, the softer aspiration forgotten. And then they laugh at what they used to do. I have sometimes thought it a pity. But that's no matter now.

Bill o' Burnt Bay knew this lad—knew his weird, sad songs, and had bellowed them in the cabin of the *Cash Down* —

"Oh, the chain 'e parted,
An' the schooner drove ashore;
An' the wives of the hands
Never seed un any more—
No more:
Never seed un no mor-or-or-ore!"

It was a song weird and sad enough for a little lad like Toby Farr to make. Before a bogie-stove in the forecastle of a schooner at anchor, Toby Farr could yarn of foul weather in a way to set the flesh of a man's back creeping with fear; but it was told of him at Jolly Harbour,

and laid to the sad songs he made, that in a pother of northeasterly weather he was no great hand for laughter.

"'Tis Toby's first season at the ice, Bill," said Jonathan. "Eh, Toby?"

"Ay, sir."

"An' gran'pa come along with you, didn't he, Toby? You wanted ol' gran'pa for company, didn't you? Eh, Toby?"

"Ay, sir."

"Isn't got no father, is you, Toby?"

"No, sir."

"Isn't got nobody but gran'pa t' fetch you up —is you? Eh, Toby?"

"I'm content, sir."

"Hear that, Bill! He's content! An' he've been doin' well out here over the side on the ice. Isn't you, Toby?"

"Is I, gran'pa?" It was a flash of hope.

"*Is* you!"

"Ay—is I, sir?" It was eager. "Is I been doin' well, sir—as you'd have me do?"

"That you is!"

"Is you tellin' me the truth, gran'pa? It isn't jus' t' hearten me, is it?"

"'Tis the truth! You is doin' better, Toby,

than your father done at your age. I never knowed a lad t' do so well first time on ice like this. An' you was all on fire t' come t' the ice, wasn't you, Toby?"

"I wanted t' come, sir."

"An' you've not repented, Toby? Mm-m?"

"No, sir." The lad stared about and sighed. "I'm glad I come, sir."

Jonathan turned to Archie with his face all in a pucker of joy.

"There's spirit, sir!" he declared.

"Ay," said Archie; "that's brave enough, God knows!"

"I been cronies with Toby, Bill," Jonathan went on, to Bill o' Burnt Bay, "ever since he was born. A ol' man like me plays with children. He've nothin' else t' do. An' I'm enjoyin' it out here at the ice with Toby. 'Tis a pleasure for a ol' man like me t' teach the young. An' I'm wonderful fond o' this here gran'son o' mine. Isn't I, Toby? Eh, lad?"

"That you is, gran'pa!" the lad agreed. "You been wonderful good t' me all my life long."

"Hear that, Bill!" Jonathan exclaimed.

The lad was mannerly and grave.

"I wisht, sir," said he, "that my conduct might win your praise."

And then Cap'n Saul called them aboard with a saucy toot of the whistle, as though they had been dawdling the day in pranks and play.

CHAPTER XXXI

In Which a Gale of Wind Almost Lays Hands on the Crew of the "Rough and Tumble," Toby Farr is Confronted With the Suggestion of Dead Men, Piled Forward Like Cord-Wood, and Archie Armstrong Joins Bill o' Burnt Bay and Old Jonathan in a Roar of Laughter

ARCHIE ARMSTRONG and Toby Farr made friends that night. The elder boy was established as the patron of the younger. Toby was aware of Archie's station—son and heir of the great Sir Archibald Armstrong; but being outport born and bred, Toby was not overawed. Before it was time to turn in he was chatting on equal terms with Archie, just as Billy Topsail had chatted, in somewhat similar circumstances, on Archie's first sealing voyage.

Toby sang songs that night, too—songs for the crew, of his own making; and he yarned for them—tales of his own invention. It occurred to Archie more than once that Toby possessed a talent that should not be lost—that something ought to be done about it, that something *must* be done about it; and Archie determined that something should be done about it—Archie was old enough to understand the power of his prospective wealth and his own responsibility with relation to it.

And that night, below, when Toby Farr was curled up asleep, Archie learned more of this queer matter of Jonathan and the lad. He learned that it was in the mind of old Jonathan Farr that he would not last long in the world—that he was wistful to have the lad hardened before the time of his departure fell. Proper enough: for of all that Jonathan had to leave the lad, which was much, when you come to think it over, he could leave him no better fortune than a store of courage and the will and skill to fend for himself.

But the ice was no fit place for Jonathan Farr—a lean, weary old dog like Jonathan Farr. Ah, well, said he, what matter? For his time was on the way, and the lad was heartened and taught in his company; and as for the frost that might bite his old flesh, and as for the winds that might chill the marrow of his old bones, it was nothing at all to suffer that much, said he, in the cause of his own son's son, who was timid, as his father had been, in youth, and his father's father before him.

"Ay," said Archie; "but the lad's too young for the ice."

"True, Archie—he's tender," said Jonathan; "but I've no certainty o' years. An' I done well with his father, Archie, at his age."

"'Twould go hard with a tender lad like Toby in time of trouble."

"No, no, Archie ——"

"He'd never live it through, Jonathan."

"Ay," Jonathan replied; "but I'm here, Archie—me! An' that's jus' what I'm here for —t' keep un safe from harm while I teaches un t' fend for hisself."

"You!" Bill o' Burnt Bay put in, in banter.

"I'm old—true," says Jonathan. "Yet I've a shot left in the locker, Bill, against a time o' need."

Next day Cap'n Saul found the herds—a patch of harps and new-whelped young. The crew killed all that day. At dusk the men were used to the slaughter, and could bat a seal and travel the ice without fear or awkwardness. There was a pretty prospect indeed of making a quick voyage of it. And this would mean a puff and bouquet of praise for Cap'n Saul in the St. John's newspapers, and a sixty dollar share in the fat for every man and lad of the crew: "*Rough and Tumble*, Cap'n Saul Galt, First Arrival. In With Thirty Thousand!"—all in big, black letters to startle folks' eyes and set the tongues of the town clacking.

It would be news of a size to make the town chatter for a fortnight; it would spread to the outports; it would give Cap'n Saul all the sealing glory of that year. There would be great stir and wonder in Water Street when Cap'n Saul went by; and there would be a lively gathering for congratulations in the office of the owners when Cap'n Saul swaggered in to report what everybody knew, that Saul Galt, of the *Rough and Tumble*, was the first of the fleet to come in with a load.

Sir Archibald Armstrong himself would be there to clap the skipper on the back.

"I congratulate you, Cap'n Saul!" he would say. "I'm proud o' ye, sir!"

Driving this way and that, and squirming along, nosing and ramming and blasting a course through the floes, the *Rough and Tumble* loaded fifteen thousand seals in a week. It was still gray weather—no wind to matter; and the sea was flat in the lakes and lanes, and the ice was abroad, and no great frost fell to scorch the crew. Bill o' Burnt Bay was master of the Third Watch—the watch of Jonathan Farr and Toby. At dawn the First Watch filed over the side, every man with a gaff and a tow-rope and a biscuit or two; and all day long they killed and sculped and towed and panned the fat—all smothered in blood.

Meanwhile the *Rough and Tumble* ran away out of sight to land the Second Watch on another field, and beyond that, then, to land the Third Watch; and then she made back through the ice to stand by and pick up the First Watch. And when she had picked up the First Watch, and stowed away the seals, and had gathered the Second Watch, it was dusk and after every night, and sometimes long after, when she got back to pick up Bill o' Burnt Bay's watch, which was the last to leave the floe.

Thus it was labour all day and sweat most of the night—torches on the pans where the sculped seal lay; and torches on deck—the decks all red and slippery with blood and fat and ice. And it looked well for them, every one—a load of fat and the first to port with it.

Toby Farr killed and sculped and towed and panned a lad's full share of the fat.

"Well, sir," said Archie, one day, "how you getting along?"

"I thrives, sir," Toby replied.

"A cock so soon!" said Bill.

"My gran'pa," says Toby, "is teachin' me."

Archie laughed.

"Is you apt?" Bill inquired.

"I've learned courage," Toby replied, "an' 'tis a hard lesson t' learn."

"God knows!" Bill agreed.

"I'll be jus' 's fit an' able 's anybody, mark me," Toby boasted, "afore this v'y'ge is out!"

"I believe you!" said Archie.

Foul weather fell with the crews on the floe—a brief northeast gale of cold wind. The floe went crunching to the southwest—jumping along with the wind like a drove of scared white rabbits. And the pans packed; and the lakes began to close—the lanes to close. Bill o' Burnt Bay gathered his watch in haste. Seals? Drop the seals! It was time for caution—quick work for crews and ship. Cap'n Saul snatched the other watches from the ice and footed it back for Bill's watch before the press nipped the *Rough and Tumble* and caught her fast; and Bill's watch was aboard before dusk, leaving the kill to drift where the wind had the will to drive it.

Cap'n Saul was proud of the smart work—smelling out a swift gale of northeasterly wind with that old foul-weather nose of his, and picking his crew from the ice with the loss of not a man. It was a narrow shave, though—narrow enough to keep a man's heart in his mouth until he got a mug of hot tea in his stomach. And that night there was talk of it below—yarns of the ice: the loss of the *Greenland's* men in a blizzard—poor, doomed men, cut off from the ship and freezing to madness and death; and of how the *Greenland* steamed into St. John's Harbour with her flag at half-mast and dead men piled forward like cord-wood.

Tales of frosty wind and sudden death—all told in whispers to saucer eyes and open mouths.

"A sad fate, Toby!" said Jonathan, to test the lad's courage. "Mm-m?"

Toby shrugged his shoulders.

"Yep," said he.

"All them poor dead men in a heap!"

"Sad enough, sir."

"Cast away in the cold an' all froze stiff!"

"Yep."

"Hard as stone!"

"Yep."

"An' piled for'ard like cord-wood!"

"Sad sight, sir. Yep."

"Oh, dear me!" said Jonathan.

Toby put a hand on the old man's shoulder. It was to hearten his grandfather's courage. And Toby smiled.

"Cheer up, gran'pa!" said he. "You isn't afeared, is you?"

"Hear that, Bill!" cried Jonathan.

Toby whistled a tune.

"Whistlin'!" said Bill. "Yet afore this v'y'ge is out ye may lie a blue corpse yourself on the ice!"

And Toby yawned.

"Yep," said he.

It was a cure. Archie and Bill and Jonathan burst into a roar of laughter. Toby was timid no longer. He could not be frightened by tales and gruesome suggestions to his imagination.

CHAPTER XXXII

In Which Archie Armstrong and Billy Topsail Say Good-bye to Toby Farr for the Present, and, Bound Down to Our Harbour with Doctor Luke, Enter Into an Arrangement, From Which Issues the Discovery of a Mysterious Letter and Sixty Seconds of Cold Thrill

WHAT happened next was the astonishing meeting of Archie Armstrong and Billy Topsail in Tom Lute's cottage on Amen Island. The rising blast of wind that threatened to interrupt Doctor Luke's passage of Ship's Run, and thus cost Terry Lute the "fiddle finger" he cherished, so dealt with the floe, at sea, where the men of the *Rough and Tumble* were at work, that Archie was cut off from return to the ship. At first the adventure wore a grave appearance; but Archie knew the coast, and was aware, also, that the land near which the *Rough and Tumble* had debarked her crew in the morning was the land of Amen Island.

That there was an hospitable settlement on

Amen Island, Cap'n Saul had told him. It was towards Amen Island, then, that his endeavour was directed, when the shifting ice cut him off from the ship and dusk caught him on the floe. And he had no great difficulty in making the shore. The floe, in the grip of the wind, drifted towards the land and came in contact with it before night fell.

Archie had a long, stumbling search for the cottages of Amen. That was the most trying aspect of his experience. In the end, however, pretty well worn out, but triumphant, he caught sight of the light in Tom Lute's cottage ; and he knocked on the door and pushed into the kitchen just when Doctor Luke, having lanced Terry Lute's finger, and having been informed that Terry Lute's fiddle was a jew's-harp, had joined Billy Topsail in the hearty laughter that the amazing disclosure excited.

It was late then. Archie and Billy and Doctor Luke were all feeling the effect of the physical labour of that stormy night; and when Billy and Archie had exchanged news in sufficient measure to ease their curiosity, and when Doctor Luke and Archie, who were old friends, had accomplished the same satisfying end, and Black Walt and his assistant had departed, and when Terry Lute and Tom Lute and Terry Lute's mother had recovered from their delight, the simple household turned in to sleep as best it could.

In the morning—which means almost immediately after dawn—Archie Armstrong insisted upon his own way. And his own way was happy and acceptable. The *Rough and Tumble* lay offshore. She was within sight from the window of Tom Lute's cottage. Undoubtedly Cap'n Saul had a searching party—probably the whole crew—out after Archie Armstrong; and undoubtedly the old man was in a fever and fury of anxiety—a fury of anxiety because, no great wind having blown, and the ice having been driven against the coast, his alarm for Archie's safety need not be great, whereas the delay caused by Archie's misadventure would surely arouse a furious impatience.

Consequently Archie sought to relieve both his anxiety and his impatience; and to this end he set out over the ice, with Billy Topsail and Doctor Luke, to board the *Rough and Tumble*, where Billy Topsail was wanting to shake the hand of his old friend, Bill o' Burnt Bay, and Archie was eager to have Doctor Luke "inspect" Toby Farr and his grandfather. It was in Archie's mind to "make a man" of Toby.

"Cap'n Saul," said Archie, by and by, "will you be sailing to the s'uth'ard?"

"A mad question!" Cap'n Saul growled.

"Yes; but, sir ——"

"Isn't you got no sense at all? How can I tell where the ice will go?"

Archie grinned.

"It wasn't very bright, sir," he admitted. "Still, Cap'n Saul, is there any chance ——"

"Why?"

"I want to go down with Doctor Luke, sir, to Our Harbour. But I don't want to be left on the coast until the mail-boat comes north. If you think you *might* be in the neighbourhood of Our Harbour, and could send a boat ashore for me, sir, I'll take a chance."

"I might," Cap'n Saul replied. "An' the way the ice sets, I think I will. Will that do ye?"

"It will, sir!"

"If the ice goes t' sea ——"

"You'll leave me. I understand that."

"I'll leave ye like a rat!"

Archie laughed.

"Billy," said he, gleefully, "I'll go south with you!" And to Cap'n Saul: "How long will you give me, sir?"

"I'll give you a week."

"Make it ten days, sir?"

"Archie," Cap'n Saul replied, "I thought you was a b'y o' some sense. How can I say a week or ten days? I'll pick you up if I can. An' that's all I'll say. What I'm here for is *swiles*. An' swiles I'll have, b'y, no matter whether you're left on the coast or not."

Archie flushed.

"Cap'n Saul, sir," said he, "I beg pardon. You see, sir, I—I ——"

Cap'n Saul clapped him on the back.

"Archie, b'y," said he, putting an arm over the boy's shoulder, "I'll pick you up if I can. An' if I can't"—Cap'n Saul accomplished a heavy wink—"there'll be some good reason why I don't. Now, you mark me!"

Upon that understanding Archie packed a seaman's bag and went back to Amen Island with Doctor Luke and Billy Topsail. First, however, he shook the hand of Bill o' Burnt Bay, and shook the hand of Toby Farr, and shook the hand of Jonathan Farr. And Billy

Topsail shook hands with them all, too. Billy Topsail liked the quality of Toby Farr. They were to go through a gale of wind together—Archie and Billy and Bill and Jonathan and little Toby Farr. And Billy and Archie were to learn more of the quality of Toby Farr—to stand awed in the presence of the courage and nobility of Jonathan Farr.

Thus it came about that Doctor Luke, Billy Topsail and Archie Armstrong, near dusk, two days later, drove Doctor Luke's dogs into Bread-and-Butter Tickle, on the way south to Doctor Luke's hospital at Our Harbour. There was sickness near by—at Round Cove and Explosion Bight; and as Doctor Luke was in haste, he was in something of a quandary. Doctor Luke's solution and immediate decision were sufficient.

Billy Topsail was to carry medicine and directions, especially directions, which had a good deal to do with the virtues of fresh air, to ease the slight trouble at Explosion Bight, and Doctor Luke would himself attend to the serious case at Round Cove, setting off at once and returning before noon of the next day, all being well.

Billy's errand was the longer; it might be two or three days before he could get back—Explosion Bight lay beyond Poor Luck Barrens—but at any rate a start for Our Harbour would be made as soon as he got back. As for Archie Armstrong, he was to kick his heels and feed the dogs at Bread-and-Butter Tickle—a prospect that he did not greatly enjoy, but was disposed to make the best of. As it turned out, the issue of the whole arrangement gave him sixty seconds of thrill that he will never forget.

In the operation of the plan, returning from Explosion Bight, where he had executed his directions, dusk of a scowling day caught Billy Topsail on the edge of the woods. And that was a grave matter—Billy Topsail was in driven haste. As the white wilderness day had drawn on, from a drab dawn to a blinding noon, and from noon to the drear, frosty approach of night, the impression of urgency, in the mystery that troubled him, grew large and whipped him faster.

When he loped from the timber into the wind, high above the sea, he was dog-tired and breathless. It was offshore weather then; a black night threatened; it was blowing in tepid gray gusts from the southwest; a flutter of wet snow was in the gale. In the pool of ghostly, leaden dark, below Spear Rock, of Yellow Head, the ice of Skeleton Arm was wrenched from the coast; and with an accumulation of Arctic bergs and drift-pans, blown in by the last nor'easter, it was sluggishly moving into the black shadows of the open sea. And having observed the catastrophe, in a swift, sweeping flash, Billy Topsail stopped dead on the ridge of Spear Rock, dismayed and confounded.

To camp on Spear Rock was no incident of his dogged intention.

Bread-and-Butter Tickle, to which a persistent, feverish impression of urgency, divined from the puzzling character of the incident of the night before, had driven Billy Topsail since the drab dawn of that day, lay across the darkening reaches of Skeleton Arm. In the snug basin, beyond the heads of the narrows, the lamps were lighted in the cottages of the place. It was a twinkling, beckoning hospitality; it invited Billy Topsail to supper and to bed—to the conclusion of his haste and to the relief of his mystification.

But on the Labrador coast, as elsewhere, the longest way round is often the shortest way home. It was two miles across Skeleton Arm to

Bread-and-Butter Tickle, on a direct line from Spear Head; it was four miles alongshore to Rattle Water Inlet, at the head of Skeleton Arm, and eight from Rattle Water to the lights of Bread-and-Butter. Billy Topsail reflected upon the discrepancy—the flurry of snow, too, and the swift approach and thick quality of the night; and having surveyed the ice, the fragments of which seemed still to be sufficiently in contact for crossing, he clambered down Spear Head to the shore of the sea.

"Can I cross?" he wondered.

After further reflection:

"I don't know," he concluded.

What mystified Billy Topsail, and drove and challenged him, as he had never been mystified and driven and challenged before, was a letter. Billy Topsail had come through the scrub timber and barrens beyond the first wild hills of Long-Age Inlet; and having came to the fork in the trail from Run-By-Guess to Poor Luck Barrens, where he was to camp for the night, he had been confronted by a new-cut stick, stoutly upright in the snow of the trail, and a flutter of red flannel rag, and a letter, snapped in the cleft head of the stick.

That the solitary wilderness of his journey should be so concerned with the outport world of that coast as to produce a letter was amazing; and that the letter should present itself, in the nick of time, where, probably, no other traveller except the mail-man had passed since the first snow fell, and that a fluttering flannel rag should declare its whereabouts, as though confidently beseeching instant conveyance to its destination, was more stimulating to Billy Topsail's reflection than mere amazement could be.

"Now," thought he, "what's this?"

It was darkly, vitally mysterious.

"'Tis the queerest thing ever I knowed!"

The letter was a folded brown paper, sealed tight, doubtless with a paste of flour and water; and it was inscribed in an illiterate scrawl: BREDNBUTR—which Billy Topsail had the wit to decipher at once. Bread-and-Butter—nobody in particular at Bread-and-Butter; anybody at all at Bread-and-Butter. Need was signified; haste was besought—a letter in a cleft stick, left to do its own errand, served by its own resources, with a fluttering red flannel rag to arrest and entreat the traveller.

Obviously it was intended for the mail-man.

But the mail-man, old Bob Likely, with his long round—the mail-man, where was he? Billy Topsail did not open the letter; it was sealed—it was an inviolate mystery. Fingering it, scrutinizing it, in astonished curiosity, he reflected, however, upon the coincidence of its immediate discovery—the tracks were fresh in the snow and the brown paper was not yet weather-stained; and so remarkable did the coincidence appear that he was presently obsessed with the impulse to fulfill it.

He pushed back his cap in bewilderment.

"Jus' seems t' me," he reflected, gravely, "as if I was *meant* t' come along an' find this letter."

It was, truly, a moving coincidence.

"I ought t' be shot," Billy Topsail determined, "if I doesn't get this here letter t' Bread-and-Butter the morrow night!"

CHAPTER XXXIII

In Which the Letter is Opened, Billy and Archie are Confronted by a Cryptogram, and, Having Exercised Their Wits, Conclude that Somebody is in Desperate Trouble

IT was a woman's doing. The signs of a woman were like print—little tracks in the snow—a woman's little foot; and the snow was brushed by a skirt. What woman? A girl? It was a romantic suggestion. Billy Topsail was old enough to respond to the appeal of chivalry. A perception of romance overwhelmed him. He was thrilled. He blushed. Reflecting, thus, his thought tinged with the fancies of romance, his chivalry was fully awakened. No; he would not open the letter. It was a woman's letter. An impulse of delicacy forbade him to intrude. Wrong? Perhaps. Yet it was a fine impulse. He indulged it. He stowed the letter away. And at dawn, still in a chivalrous glow, he set out for Bread-and-Butter Tickle, resolved to deliver the letter that night; and he was caught by dusk on the ridge of Spear Head, with a flurry of wet snow in the wind and the night threatening thick.

Having come to the edge of the moving ice, Billy Topsail looked across to the lights of Bread-and-Butter.

"Might 's well," he decided.

Between Spear Head and Bread-and-Butter Tickle, that night, Billy Topsail had a nip-and-tuck time of it. It was dark. Snow intermittently obscured his objective. The ice was fragmentary—driving and revolving in a slow wind. It was past midnight when he hauled down the heads of Bread-and-Butter and knocked Archie Armstrong out of bed.

"Archie," said he, "I found a queer thing."

Archie's sleepiness vanished.

"Queer?" he demanded, eagerly. "Something queer? What is it?"

"'Tis a letter."

"A letter! Where is it?"

Billy related the circumstances of the discovery of the letter. Then he said:

"'Tis a sealed letter. I wants t' show it t' Doctor Luke."

"He's not back."

"Not back? That's queer!"

"Oh, no," said Archie, easily; "the case has turned out to be more serious than he thought and has detained him. Where's the letter?"

Billy gave the letter to Archie.

"Bread-and-Butter," Archie read. "No other address. That *is* queer. What shall we do about it?"

"I don't know," Billy replied. "What do *you* say?"

"I say open it," said Archie, promptly.

"Would you?"

"There's nothing else to do. Open it, of course! It is addressed to Bread-and-Butter. Well, we're in Bread-and-Butter. Doctor Luke isn't here. If he were, he'd open it. There is something in this letter that somebody ought to know at once. I'm going to open it."

"All right," Billy agreed.

Archie opened the letter and stared and frowned and pursed his lips.

"What does it say?" said Billy.

"I can't make it out. Have a try yourself. Here—read it if you can."

Billy was confronted by a cryptogram:

Dokr com quk pops goncras im ferd

"What do you make of it?" said Archie.

"I'm not much of a hand at readin'," Billy replied; "but I knows that first word there or I misses my guess."

"What is it?"

"D-O-K-R. That means what it sounds like. It means *Doctor*."

Archie exclaimed.

"That's it!" said he. "And the second word's plain. C-O-M—that's *Come*."

"'*Doctor, come*,'" said Billy.

"Right. Somebody's in trouble. Deep trouble, too. The third word is *Quick*. '*Doctor, come quick*.' We're right so far. P-O-P-S. What's that?"

"It means *Father*."

"Right. '*Doctor, come quick. Pop's*——' What now? 'G-O-N-C-R-A-S.' What in the world is that? It must be a kind of sickness. Can't you guess it, Billy?"

Billy puzzled.

"G-O-N-C-R-A-S. I don't know what it means."

"Anyhow," Archie put in, "the next word must be *I'm*. Don't you think so, Billy? No? Looks like that. Hum-m! Look here, Billy—what's F-E-R-D? What does it sound like?"

"Sounds like *feared*."

"Of course it does! That's right! '*I'm afeared*.' Billy, this is a pretty serious matter. Why should the writer of this be afraid? Eh? You think a woman wrote the letter? Well, she's afraid of something. And that something must be the sort of sickness her father has. Shake your nut, Billy. What sort of sickness could she be afraid of?"

"G-O-N-C-R-A-S. Gon-cras."

"Gon-cras. Gon-cras. Gon-cras."

"*Gone*," Billy suggested.

"*Crazy!*" cried Archie.

"Right!" said Billy.

"We've got it!" Archie exulted. "'*Doctor, come quick. Pop's gone crazy. I'm afeared*.' That's the message. What shall we do?"

"We can't do anything now."

"How's the ice on the Arm, Billy?"

"Movin' out. A man couldn't cross now. I barely made it."

"Will the Arm be free in the morning?"

"No; it will not. The Arm will be fit for neither foot nor punt in the morning. T' get t' Poor Luck Barrens a man would have t' skirt the Arm t' Rattle Water an' cross the stream."

"We'll have to do something, Billy. We can't leave that poor girl alone with a madman."

"We'll tell Doctor Luke ——"

"Yes; but what if Doctor Luke isn't back in the morning?"

"We'll go ourselves."

Archie started.

"Go?" he inquired, blankly. "Go *where?* We don't know where this letter came from. It isn't signed."

"Ah, well," said Billy, "somebody in Bread-and-Butter will know. Let's turn in, Archie. If we're t' take the trail the morrow, we must have rest."

And they turned in.

CHAPTER XXXIV

In Which Archie and Billy Resolve Upon a Deed of Their Own Doing, and are Challenged by Ha-Ha Shallow of Rattle Water

NEITHER boy slept very much. In Samuel Jolly's spare bed (it was called a spare bed)—where they had tumbled in together—they did more talking than sleeping. And that could not be helped. It was a situation that appealed to the imagination of two chivalrous boys—a woman all alone on Poor Luck Barrens with a madman. When morning came they were up with the first peep of the light; and they were in a nervous condition of such a sort that neither would hesitate over a reckless chance if it should confront them in an attempt to help the writer of the letter of the cleft stick.

"Who is she?" Archie demanded of Samuel Jolly.

"Jinny Tulk, sir—Trapper George's daughter."

"How does she come to be at Poor Luck Barrens?"

"Trapper George has a trappin' tilt there, sir.

They're both from this harbour. They goes trappin' on Poor Luck Barrens in the winter. Jinny keeps house for her pop."

"All alone?"

"Ay, sir; there's nobody livin' near."

Archie turned to Billy.

"Look here, Billy," said he, anxiously, "we've *got* to go. I can't bear it here—with that poor girl all alone——"

"Doctor Luke——"

"We can't wait for Doctor Luke."

"That's jus' what I was goin' t' say," said Billy. "We'll leave word for Doctor Luke that we've gone. He can follow. An' when we gets there, we can keep Trapper George quiet until Doctor Luke comes."

"When shall we start?"

"Now!"

Outbound from Bread-and-Butter, fortified with instructions, Billy Topsail and Archie Armstrong made along the shore of Skeleton Arm, by the long trail, and were halted before noon at Rattle Water. The ice had gone out of Rattle Water. At the ford the stream was deep, swift, bitter cold—manifestly impassable; and above, beyond

Serpent Bend, the water of Ha-ha Shallow, which was the alternative crossing, was in a turmoil, swelling and foaming over the boulders in its wide, shallow bed.

Except where the current eddied, black, flecked with froth, Ha-ha Shallow was not deep. A man might cross—submerged somewhat above the knees, no more; but in the clinging grip and tug of the current his footing would be delicately precarious, and the issue of a misstep, a stumble, a lost balance, would be a desperate chance, with the wager heavily on grim Death.

It was perilous water—the noisy, sucking white rush of it, frothing over the boulders, and running, icy cold, in choppy, crested waves, where the channel was a bed of stones and gravel. Yet the path to the tilt at Poor Luck Barrens lay across and beyond Ha-ha Shallow of Rattle Water.

Billy Topsail and Archie Armstrong surveyed the rapids in a dubious silence.

"Hum!" Archie coughed.

Billy Topsail chuckled.

"You've no fancy for the passage?" he inquired.

"I have not. Have you?"

"I don't hanker for it, Archie. No, sir—not me!"

"Can it be done?"

"No, b'y."

"No; it can't be done," Archie declared. "You're right."

They stared at the tumultuous stream.

"Come along," said Archie, with decision, his teeth set; "we'll try that ice below again."

Below Ha-ha Shallow, where the stream dropped into a deep, long pool, lying between low cliffs, fringed with the spruce of that stunted wilderness, Rattle Water was bridged with ice. There had been flood water in the early spring break-up—a rush of broken ice, a jam in Black Pool, held by the rocks of its narrow exit; and the ice had been caught and sealed by the frosts of a swift spell of bitter weather.

The subsidence of Rattle Water, when the ice below Black Pool ran off with the current into the open reaches of Skeleton Arm, had left the jam suspended. It was a bridge from shore to shore, lifted a little from the water; but in the sunshine and thaw and warm rain of the subsequent interval it had gone rotten. Its heavy collapse was imminent.

And of this Billy Topsail and Archie had made sure on the way up-stream from the impassable ford to the impassable white water of Ha-ha Shallow. The ice-bridge could not be crossed. It awaited the last straw—a rain, a squall of wind, another day of sunshine and melting weather. Billy had ventured, on pussy-feet, and had withdrawn, threatened by a crack, his hair on end.

A second trial of the bridge had precisely the same result. Archie cast a stone. It plumped through.

"Soft 's cheese," said Billy.

Another stone was cast.

"Hear that, Billy?"

"Clean through, Archie."

"Yes; clean through. It's all rotten. We can't cross. Give me a hand. I'll try it."

With a hand from Billy Topsail, Archie let himself slip over the edge of the cliff to an anxious footing on the ice.

He waited—expectant.

"Cautious, Archie!" Billy warned.

Nothing happened.

"Cautious!" Billy repeated. "You'll drop through, b'y!"

Archie took one step—and dropped, crashing, with a section of the bridge, which momentarily floated his weight. Billy caught his hand, as the ice disintegrated under his feet, and dragged him ashore.

"It can't be done," said Archie.

"No, b'y; it can't."

"We'll try Ha-ha Shallow again. We've *got* to get across."

A moment, however, Archie paused. A startling possibility possessed his imagination. It was nothing remote, nothing vague; it was real, concrete, imminent. Standing on the brink of the rock at the point where the ice-bridge began, he contemplated the chances of Rattle Water. With a crossing of Ha-ha Shallow immediately in prospect, there was something for affrighted reflection in the current below. And the suggestion was vivid and ugly.

There the water was flowing black, spread with creamy puffs of foam; and it ran swift and deep, in strong, straight lines, as it approached the Black Pool ice and vanished beneath. There was a space between the ice and the fallen current—not much: two feet, perhaps; but it occurred to Archie, with sudden, shocking force, that two feet were too much. And the deep, oily, adherent flow of the current, and the space between the ice and the water, and the cavernous shadow beneath the ice, and the gurgle and lapping of the pool, made the flesh of his back uneasy.

"A nasty fix," he observed.

"What's that, Archie?"

"If a man lost his feet in the current."

"He'd come down like a chip."

"He would. And he'd slip under the ice. Watch these puffs of foam. What would happen to a man under there, Billy?"

"He'd drown in the pool. He couldn't get out."

"Right, Billy," Archie agreed, shortly. "He'd drown in the pool. He couldn't get out. The current would hold him in there. Come along."

"Shall we try it, Archie?"

"We'll look it over."

"An' if we think ——"

"Then we'll do it!"

Billy laughed.

"Archie," said he, "I—I—I *likes* you!"

"Shucks!" said Archie.

Archie walked the length of Ha-ha Shallow, from the swift water above Black Pool to Loon

Lake, and returned, still searching the rapid for a good crossing, to a point near the Black Pool ice, where a choppy ripple promised a shallow, gravelled bottom. The stream was wide, shelving slowly from the shore—it was prattling water; but there was a fearsomely brief leeway of distance between the stretch of choppy ripple and the deep rush of the current as it swept into the shadows under the Black Pool ice.

Directly below the ripple, Rattle Water narrowed and deepened; nearing Black Pool, the banks were steep, and above the rising gorge, which the banks formed, and running the length of it, the current swelled over a scattering of slimy boulders and swirled around them. It was a perilous place to be caught. In the gravel-bottomed ripple, the water was too swift, too deep, for an overbalanced boy to regain his feet; and in the foaming, hurrying, deeper water below, the rough drift to Black Pool was inevitable: for the boulders were water-worn and round, and the surface was as slippery as grease with slime.

Having stared long enough at the alluring stretch of choppy ripple, Archie Armstrong came to a conclusion.

CHAPTER XXXV

In Which Billy Topsail Takes His Life in His Hands and Ha-Ha Shallow Lays Hold of It With the Object of Snatching It Away

"WELL," said Archie, "I'll try it."

"You won't!" said Billy.

"I will!"

"You won't!"

Archie looked Billy in the eye.

"Why not?" he inquired.

"I'm goin' t' try it myself."

"You're not!"

"I am!"

Both boys burst into a laugh. It was an amiable thing to do. And there could have been no better preparation for the work in hand.

"Look here, Billy ——" Archie began.

"No," Billy insisted; "it won't do. You haves your way always, Archie. An' now I'm goin' t' have my turn at it. I'll try it first. An' if I gets across you can follow."

"You might stumble."

"I know that."

"Look here, Billy ——"

"No, no, b'y! I'm goin' first. I won't make a fool o' myself. We got t' get across this stream if we can. An' we've got t' get on t' Poor Luck Barrens. But I won't make a fool o' myself, Archie. I promise you that. I'll go jus' as far as I can. I'll go with care—jus' as far as I can. An' if 'tis no use tryin' any more, I'll come back. That's a promise. I'll come back. An' then ——"

"Ay, Billy?"

"I'll try somewhere else."

"Billy," said Archie, "I—I—I *likes* you!"

"Stop your jawin'!" said Billy.

Then Archie said:

"If you fall in the current I'll pull you out, Billy. You trust *me*."

Billy spoke gravely:

"You'll do no such thing."

"What!" cried Archie. "Not try to save ——"

"No."

"Why, Billy," Archie protested, "you're just plain foolish to ask me not to ——"

"No," said Billy, again; "it isn't foolish. I won't have it."

Archie said nothing.

"Now," said Billy, "I'll try my hand at it."

The gravity and untoward chances of the attempt were not ignored. Both boys were aware of them. A simple thing to splash into the first shallow inches of Rattle Water and there deliberate an advance—true enough; but Billy Topsail was in earnest about crossing. He would venture far and perilously before he turned back—venture to the brink of safety, and tentatively, definitely into the dragging grip of the deeper current beyond. A boy who proposes to go as far as he can is in the way of overreaching himself. Beyond his utmost, whatever his undertaking, lies a mocking, entreating temptation to his courage—an inch or two more.

"Billy!" said Archie.

"Ay?"

"Do you think that if you fall in the current I'll stand by and ——"

"I hopes you will, Archie. If I loses my feet, I goes down-stream. That's plain. No man could catch his feet in that water. An' if I goes all the way down-stream, I goes clean under Black Pool ice. An' if I goes under Black Pool ice, I can't get out, because the current will hold me there. That's plain, too. You couldn't pull me out o' the stream. If you could do that, I could get out alone. You'd jus' go down with me. So you leave me go."

"Billy, I ——"

"Oh, I isn't goin' t' fall anyhow, Archie. An' if I does, I'll make a fight. If I can grab anything on the way down; an' if I can hang in the stream, we'll talk it over again."

"Billy ——"

"That's all, Archie."

With that Billy Topsail, the pack of food on his back (since if he won the other bank he must have sustenance for the chances of his journey to Poor Luck Barrens), waded into the water.

Presently Billy Topsail was ankle deep in the stream. The water foamed to his calves. Suspense aggravated him. He splashed on—impatient to come to the crisis that challenged him. It was a stony bed—loose, round, slippery stones; and a stone turned—and Billy Topsail tottered in the deeper suck of the current. It was nothing to regain his balance in that shallow. And he pushed on. But by and by—time being relative to suspense, it seemed a long, long time to Archie Armstrong, waiting on the snowy bank—by and by Billy Topsail was knee deep and anxiously engaged; and mid-stream, where the ripple was dancing down in white-capped, choppy waves, was still proportionately far distant.

Billy paused, then, to settle his feet. The footing was treacherous; the water was white to his thighs—the swift, dizzy, noisy passage was confusing. For a new advance he halted to make good his grip of the bottom and to brace and balance himself against the insistent push of the current.

Archie shouted:

"You're doing fine, Billy!"

In the bawling rush of the stream it was hard to hear Archie. Still, Billy heard. And he nodded—but did not dare to turn.

"Go slow," Archie called, "and you'll make it!"

Billy thought so too. He was doing well—it seemed a reasonable expectation. And he ventured his right foot forward and established it. It was slow, cautious work, thrusting through that advance, feeling over the bottom and finding a fixed foundation; and dragging the left foot forward, in resistance to the current, was as slow and as difficult. A second step, accomplished with effort; a third, achieved at greater risk; a fourth, with the hazard still more delicate—and Billy Topsail paused again.

It was deeper. The broken waves washed his thighs; the heavy body of the water was above his knees; he was wet to the waist with spray; and in the deeper water, by the law of displacement, he had lost weight. The water tended to lift him: the impulse was up to the surface—the pressure down-stream. In this respect the current was like a wrestler who lifts his opponent off his feet before he flings him down.

And in the meantime the current tightened its hold.

CHAPTER XXXVI

In Which Ha-Ha Shallow is Foiled, Archie Armstrong Displays Swift Cunning, of Which He is Well Aware, and Billy Topsail, Much to His Surprise, and not Greatly to His Distaste, is Kissed by a Lady of Poor Luck Barrens

ANOTHER advance of the right foot; an increased depth of two inches; a sudden, upward thrust of the water; a rolling stone: Billy Topsail tottered—struggled for balance, like a man on a tight-rope, and caught and held it; but in the wrenching effort his pack had shifted and disturbed his natural poise. He faced up-stream, feet spread, body bent, arms extended; and in this awkward posture, at a disadvantage, he swayed dangerously, incommoded by the pack, his legs quivering in the current.

Deliberately, then, Billy contorted himself until the pack slipped from his shoulder to its place on his back; and upright again, established once more, he dragged his left foot by inches against the current, set it above the right, forced it into place, and turned to face the opposite shore.

He was fairly mid-stream, now. Another confident, successful step—a moment more of cool behaviour and intelligent procedure—and the grip of the current would begin to fail.

All this while the tumbling water had worked its inevitable effect. It was noisy; it ran swift; it troubled Billy Topsail—the speed and clatter of it. And he was now confused and dizzy. Now, too, he was conscious of the roar of the stream below. More clamorously, more vividly, it asserted itself—reiterated and magnified its suggestion of disaster. It could not be ignored. Billy Topsail abstracted his attention. It returned to the menace.

There it was—the roar of the stream below: the deep, narrow rush of it, swelling over the boulders, curling around them, plunging irresistibly towards the Black Pool ice, and vanishing into the stifling gloom beneath, in a swift, black, silent stream, flecked with creamy puffs of foam. A misstep, a false stone, a lost balance—a man would then drift fast and helpless, bruised by the bottom, flung against the boulders and stunned, smothered by the water, cast into Black Pool and left to sink in still water. It was the logical incident of failure.

Aware of the cumulative effect of fear, conscious of the first creeping paralysis of it, Billy Topsail instantly determined upon the next step. It must be taken—it must be taken at once. Already the weakness and confusion of terror was a crippling factor to be dealt with. He must act—venture. He moved in haste; there was a misstep, an incautious faith in the foothold, a blind chance taken—and the current caught him, lifted him, tugged at him, and he lost his feet, flung his arms in the air, toppled over, drifted off with the current, submerged, and was swept like driftwood into the deep rush below.

He rose, gasped, sank—came breathless to the surface; and self-possessed again, and fighting for life against hope, instinctively, but yet with determined intelligence, grasping breath when he could and desperately seeking handhold, foothold—fighting thus he was dragged a bruising course through the narrowing channel towards Black Pool and at last momentarily arrested his drift with a failing grip of a boulder.

Archie Armstrong ran down-stream. No expedient was in his horrified mind. The impulse was to plunge in and rescue Billy if he could. That was all. But the current was swifter than he; he was outstripped—stumbling along the rocky, icy shore. When he came abreast of Billy, who was still clinging to the rock in mid-stream, he did plunge in; but he came at once to a full stop, not gone a fathom into the current, and stood staring.

Billy Topsail could not catch the bottom in the lee of the rock. Even there the current was too strong, the depth of water too great, the lee too narrow, the rock too small for a wide, sufficient backwater. Black Pool was within twenty fathoms. Billy's clutch was breaking. In a moment he would be torn away. Yet there was a moment—a minute or more of opportunity. And having assured himself of this grace, Archie Armstrong splashed ashore, without a word or a sign, scaled the bank and ran down-stream to the bridge of Black Pool ice.

The bridge was rotten. It was rotten from bank to bank. It would not bear the weight of a man. Archie Armstrong knew it. Its fall was imminent. It awaited the last straw—a dash of rain, a squall of wind. The ice was thick; there was a foot of it. And the bridge was heavy; its attachment to the low cliffs was slight; in a day—next day, perhaps—it would fall of its own weight, lie inert in the pool, drift slowly away to the open reaches of Skeleton Arm and drive to sea.

Archie Armstrong, hanging by his hands from the edge of the low cliff, broke a great fragment from the rock and thus reduced the stability of the whole; and hanging from the edge of the same low cliff, a few fathoms below, grasping the roots of the spruce, he broke a second fragment loose with his weight—a third and a fourth. And the structure collapsed. It fell in thick, spacious fragments on the quiet water of the pool, buoyant and dry, and covered the face of the water, held imprisoned by the rocks of the narrow exit.

When Billy Topsail came drifting down, Archie Armstrong, waiting on the ice, helped him out and ashore.

"Better build a fire, Archie," said Billy, presently.

"I'm doing that very thing, Billy."

"Thanks, Archie."

"Cold, b'y?"

"I'll take no harm from the wettin'."

"Harm! A hardy kid like you! I laugh!"

Billy grinned.

"When I'm rested," said he, "I'll wring out my clothes. By the time we've had a snack o' soggy grub I'll be dry. An' then we'll go on."

"On it is!"

Billy looked up.

"Archie," said he, "that was marvellous—clever!"

"Clever?" inquired Archie. "What was clever?"

And Archie Armstrong grinned. He knew well enough what was clever.

Nobody was mad at Poor Luck Barrens. But somebody was in a raving delirium of fever. And that was big George Tulk—Trapper George of Bread-and-Butter Tickle. It was a tight little tilt on the edge of the timber—winter quarters: a log shanty, with a turf roof, deep in a drift of snow, to which a rising cloud of smoke attracted the attention of Archie and Billy Topsail. No; what was alarming at Poor Luck Barrens was not a frenzy of insanity—it was the delirium of pneumonia.

Jinny Tulk was glad enough to receive the help of Billy Topsail and Archie Armstrong.

By and by Billy asked:

"Was it you put the letter in the cleft stick?"

Jinny smiled.

"Ay," said she.

"I found it," said Billy.

With that Jinny Tulk kissed Billy Topsail before he could stop her. She was old enough for that; and she was so wholesome and pretty that when Billy had reflected upon the incident he determined that he would not try to stop her should she attempt it again.

"How'd you like it?" Archie teased him, privately, when Doctor Luke had arrived and Trapper George was resting.

Billy blushed.

"'Twasn't so awful," was his stout reply.

Archie burst out laughing. Billy blushed again. Then he, too, laughed.

"I 'low I got my reward," said he.

By that time Trapper George was doing well. Doctor Luke was watchfully at work. And Doctor Luke and Jinny Tulk, with the help of a spell of frosty weather and an abundance of healing fresh air, and assisted by the determined constitution of Trapper George Tulk himself, who had formed the fixed habit of surviving adverse conditions—Doctor Luke and Jinny

Tulk worked an improvement, which passed presently into a state of convalescence and ultimately became a cure. It was no easy matter. Trapper George Tulk put one foot over the border—took a long look into the final shadows. But Doctor Luke was a good fighter. And he happened to win.

CHAPTER XXXVII

In Which Archie Armstrong Rejoins the "Rough and Tumble," With Billy Topsail for Shipmate, and They Seem Likely to be Left on the Floe, While Toby Farr, With the Gale Blowing Cold as Death and Dark Falling, Promises to Make a Song About the Ghosts of Dead Men, but is Entreated Not to Do So

ARCHIE ARMSTRONG and Billy Topsail did not wait with Doctor Luke at Poor Luck Barrens until the cure of Trapper George was accomplished. In view of Archie's wish to return to St. John's with Cap'n Saul aboard the *Rough and Tumble*, it was arranged that the boys should go back to Bread-and-Butter Tickle alone, and thence down the coast to Our Harbour, as best they could manage, carrying news of Doctor Luke's detention and the cause of it. They were sorry to say good-bye to Doctor Luke; and Doctor Luke was sorry to say good-bye to them. When the time came, Billy Topsail, who had come to love and respect the man for his warm qualities and the work that he did, sought for words to express his feeling and his thanks; but being a simple, robust fellow, not accustomed to the frank expression of feeling, not used to conventional forms, he could manage but poorly. Archie Armstrong would have been ready, fluent, and sincere in the same situation. But Billy Topsail could only stutter and flush and come to an awkward full stop.

What Billy wanted to say was clear enough in his own mind. He had been with Doctor Luke a good deal. They had been in tight places together. But it was not that. "Tight places" are only relative, after all; what is an adventure in one quarter of the world may be a mild incident in another. And that Billy Topsail and Doctor Luke had been in danger together was not particularly impressive: Billy Topsail was used to danger—to peril of that sort—and had grown to regard it as among the commonplaces of life.

That aspect of his experience with Doctor Luke to which Billy Topsail had responded was the habit of service—the instant, willing, efficient answer to the call of helpless need. Indeed, Doctor Luke appeared to Billy Topsail to be a very great man—the greatest man, in his personality and life, Billy Topsail had ever known, not excepting Sir Archibald Armstrong. And Billy Topsail had come definitely to the conclusion that what he wanted to do with his life was precisely what Doctor Luke was doing with his.

It was this that he wanted to tell Doctor Luke; and it was this that he failed to tell him.

"Good-bye, sir," he said.

"Good-bye, Billy."

"Th-th-thanks, sir."

"Thanks?" cried Doctor Luke. "For what, Billy? *I'm* the debtor."

"Th-th-thanks, sir."

"Thank *you*, Billy, boy, for your most excellent company."

And so Billy and Archie left Doctor Luke at Poor Luck Barrens—hard at work and happy in his work. They made Bread-and-Butter Tickle; they travelled down the coast without incident; they shook hands with Teddy Brisk, who was still telling his adventures on the ice-floe, his leg as sound as any leg; and they came safe to Our Harbour, where they waited until Cap'n Saul put in with the *Rough and Tumble*. And then Archie would hear of nothing but Billy's company to St. John's—Billy *must* go to St. John's, and he *would* go to St. John's on the *Rough and Tumble*, ecod, or Archie would put him in irons and carry him there! Billy had no sound objection. From St. John's he could travel easily to his home at Ruddy Cove and arrive there long before the Labrador mail-boat would be north on her first voyage.

And so the boys boarded the *Rough and Tumble* together, fell in with Bill o' Burnt Bay, Jonathan Farr and little Toby once more, and put to sea. The *Rough and Tumble* was not loaded; she had more seals to kill and stow away, and Cap'n Saul was resolved to "put back loaded" —a desirable end towards which his active crew, in conjunction with his own sealing wisdom, was fast approaching.

"I'll load in a week!" he boasted.

And then ——

Sunday, then—and that a brooding day. It was a dull, dragging time. Not a gaff was out, not a gun; not a man put foot on the floe. The *Rough and Tumble* killed no seals. It was not the custom. All that day she lay made fast to the ice, fretting for midnight. Cap'n Saul kept to his cabin. Time and quiet weather went wasting away. Quiet weather—quiet enough that day: a draught of westerly wind blowing, the sky overcast and blank, and a flurry of snow in the afternoon, which failed, before dusk, a black, still midnight drawing on.

On the first stroke of the midnight bell, for which he had waited since the dawn of that dull day, Cap'n Saul popped out of the cabin, like a jack-in-the-box, and stamped the bridge, growling and bawling his orders, in a week-day temper, until he had dropped the First Watch, and was under way through the floe, a matter of twenty miles, to land the Second Watch and the Third—feeling a way through the lanes.

Before dawn Bill o' Burnt Bay's watch, with Archie and Billy Topsail, was on the ice. Cap'n Saul put back to stand by the First Watch. Black dark yet. It was bleak on the floe! They shivered in the frost and dark. And the light lagged, as the light will, when it is waited for. It was a sad dawn. A slow glower and lift of thin, gray light: no warmth of colour in the east—no rosy flush and glow. When day broke, at last, the crew made into the herds, mad to be warm, and began to kill. Still, it was done without heart. There was less blithe slaughter, that day, than unseemly brooding and weather-gazing. It was a queer thing, too. There was no alarm of foul weather that any man could see.

A drear, gray day it was, day drawing near noon. Archie and Billy always remembered that. Yet there was no frost to touch a man's heart, no need to cower and whine in the wind, no snow to make a man afraid. A scowl in the northeast—a low, drab, sulky sky, mottled with blue-black and smoky white. They recalled it afterwards. But that was all. And Bill o' Burnt Bay fancied, then, with the lives of his crew in mind, that the weather quarter was doubtless in a temper, but no worse, and was no more than half-minded to kick up a little pother of trouble before day ran over the west.

And Bill was at ease about that.

"She'll bide as she is," he thought, "'til Cap'n Saul gets back."

Bill o' Burnt Bay was wrong. It came on to blow. The wind jumped to the northwest with a nasty notion of misbehaviour. It was all in a moment. A gust of wind, cold as death, went swirling past. They chilled to the bones in it. And then a bitter blast of weather came sweeping down. The floe began to pack and drive. Bill o' Burnt Bay gathered and numbered his watch. And then they waited for the ship. No sign. And the day turned thick. Dusk fell before its time. It was not yet midway of the afternoon. And the wind began to buffet and bite. It began to snow, too. And it was a frosty cloud of snow. It blinded—it stifled. It was flung out of the black northwest like flour from a shaken sack.

The men were afraid. They knew that weather. It was a blizzard. There was a night of mortal peril in it. There might be a night and a day—a day and two nights. And they knew what would happen to them if Cap'n Saul failed to find them before the pack nipped him and the night shut down. It had happened before to lost crews. It would happen again. Men gone stark mad in the wind—the floe strewn with drifted corpses. They had heard tales. And now they had visions. Dead men going into port—ship's flag at half-mast, and dead men going into port, frozen stiff and blue, and piled forward like cord-wood.

"I'll make a song about this," said Toby Farr.

"A song!" Archie Armstrong exclaimed.

"'Tis about the gray wraiths o' dead men that squirm in the night."

"I'd not do it!" Jonathan protested.

"They drift like snow in the black wind," said Toby.

"Ah, no!" said Jonathan. "I'd make no songs the night about dead men an' wraiths."

"Ay, but I'm well started ——"

"No, lad!"

"I've a bit about cold fingers an' the damp touch ——"

"I'd not brood upon that."

"An it please you, sir ——"

"No."

"Ah, well," Toby agreed, "I'll wait 'til I'm cozy an' warm aboard ship."

"That's better," said Archie.

Billy Topsail shuddered. Toby's imagination —ghosts and dead men—had frightened him.

"It is!" he declared.

CHAPTER XXXVIII

In Which the Wind Blows a Tempest, Our Heroes are Lost on the Floe, Jonathan Farr is Encased in Snow and Frozen Spindrift, Toby Strangely Disappears, and an Heroic Fight for Life is Begun, Wrapped in Bitter Dark

IT is well known on this coast, from Cape Race to Norman and the Labrador harbours, what happened to Cap'n Saul that night. It was vast, flat, heavy ice, thick labour for the ship, at best—square miles of pans and fields. In the push of the northwest gale, blowing down, all at once, with vigour and fury, from a new quarter, the big pans shifted and revolved. The movement was like that of a waltz—slow dancers, revolving in a waltz. And then the floe closed. And what was a clear course in the morning was packed ice before dusk.

When the day began to foul, Cap'n Saul snatched up the First Watch, where he was standing by, and came driving down after Bill o' Burnt Bay's watch. It was too late. The ice caught him. And there was no shaking free.

The men on the floe glimpsed the ship—the bulk of the ship and a cloud of smoke; but Cap'n Saul caught no glimpse of them—a huddle of poor men wrapped in snow and dusk.

A blast of the gale canted the *Rough and Tumble* until her bare yards touched the floe and Cap'n Saul had a hard time to save her alive from the gale. And that was the measure of the wind. It blew a tempest. Rescue? No rescue. The men knew that. A rescue would walk blind—stray and blow away like leaves. They must wait for clear weather and dawn.

There had been Newfoundlanders in the same hard case before. The men knew what to do.

"Keep movin'!"

"No sleep!"

"Stick t'gether!"

"Nobody lie down!"

"Fetch me a buffet, some o' you men, an I gets sleepy."

"I gives any man leave t' beat me."

"Where's Tom Land?"

"Here I is!"

"I say, Tom—Long George gives any man leave t' beat un black an' blue!"

And a laugh at that.

LIKE LOST BEASTS

"Mind the blow-holes!"

"An a man gets wet, he'll freeze solid."

"No sleep!"

"Keep movin'!"

They kept moving to keep warm. And even they larked. Tag, whilst they could see to chase—and a sad leap-frog. And they wrestled and scuffled until it was black dark and the heart went out of them all. And then they wandered, with no lee to shelter them—a hundred and seventy-three men, stamping and stumbling in the wind, clinging to life, hour after hour, and waiting for the dawn, bitten by frost and near stifled by snow. It was gnawing cold. Twelve below—it was afterwards said. And that's bitter weather. It bit through to the bones and heart. And what they wore to withstand it—no great-coats, to hamper the kill, but only jackets and caps and mitts.

The floe was flat and bare to the gale. Nobody knows the pitch of the wind. It was a full tempest. That much is known. And it stung and cut and strove to wrest them from their feet and whisk them away. And there they were—in the grip of the wind, stripped to the strength they had, like lost beasts, and helpless to fend any more. Billy Topsail saw young Simeon Tutt, of Whoopin' Harbour, trip and stagger and fall at his feet; and before Billy could lay hands on him to save him, the wind blew him away, like a leaf, and he was never seen again, but driven into a lake of water in the dark, it was thought, and there perished.

By and by Archie and Billy stumbled on old Jonathan Farr of Jolly Harbour. It was long past midnight then. And they saw no lad with him. Where was Toby?

"That you, Jonathan?" said Archie.

"'Tis I, Archie."

"You living yet?"

"No choice. I got t' live."

"Where's Toby?" said Billy.

"The lad's ——"

It was hard to hear. The old man's words jumped away with the wind. And still the boys saw no lad.

"What say?" said Billy. "I don't see Toby. Where is he?"

"In my lee," Jonathan replied. "He's restin'."

There stood old Jonathan Farr, in the writhing gloom of that night, stiff and still and patient as the dead, with his back to the gale, plastered with snow and frozen spindrift, his shoulders humped and his head drawn in like a turtle. It was bitter dark—yet not as black as the grave. It is never that on the floe. And the wind streamed past, keen as a blade with frost, thick with crisp snow, and clammy with the spray it caught up from the open lakes and flung off in sheets and mist.

Dead bodies lying roundabout then—the boys had stumbled over the dead as they walked. Young men, sprawled stiff, hard as ice to the bones, lying stark in the drifts—Big Sam Tiller, of Thank-the-Lord, he that whipped Paddy of Linger Tickle, in White Bay, when the fleet was trapped by the floe in the Year of the Small Haul, was dead by that time; and Archie had found little Dickie Ring, of Far-Away Cove, dead in his elder brother's dead arms—they were pried apart with a crowbar when the time came.

Yet there stood old Jonathan Farr, cased in snow and ice, with the life warm in him—making a lee for little Toby. And Toby was snuggled up to his grandfather, his face close—sheltered and rested from the gale, as much as might be.

Billy Topsail bent down.

"How does you?" says he.

Toby put his head out from its snug harbour, and spoke, in a passion, as though Billy had wronged him, and then ducked back from the smother of wind and snow.

"My gran'pa takes care o' *me!*" he flashed.

"Will you save him, Jonathan?" Archie asked.

"I've a shot in the locker, Archie," Jonathan replied. "I'll save un alive."

Out flashed Toby's head; and he tugged at his grandfather—and bawled up.

"Is I doin' well?" he wanted to know.

"You is!"

"Is I doin' as well as my father done at my age?"

"You is! Is you rested?"

"Ay, sir."

"Full steam ahead!" said Jonathan. With that they bore away—playing a game. And Jonathan was the skipper and Toby was the wheelman and engine. "Port!" bawled Jonathan. And "Starboard your helm!" And Billy and Archie lost sight of them in the dark.

CHAPTER XXXIX

In Which One Hundred and Seventy-Three Men of the "Rough and Tumble" are Plunged in the Gravest Peril of the Coast, Wandering Like Lost Beasts, and Some Drop Dead, and Some are Drowned, and Some Kill Themselves to be Done With the Torture They Can Bear No Longer

THEY kept close, a hundred and seventy-three living men, to start with, and then God knew how many!—kept close for comfort and safety; and they walked warily, drunk and stupid in the wind, in dread of lakes and blow-holes and fissures of water, and in living fear of crusts of snow, wind-cast over pitfalls. And they died fast in the dark. In Archie Armstrong's tortured mind childish visions of hell were revived—the swish and sad complaint of doomed souls, winging round and round and round in a frozen dark. It was like that, he thought.

Dawn delayed. It was night forever; and the dark was peopled—the throng stirred, and was not visible; and from the black wraiths of men, moving roundabout, never still, all driven round and round by the torture of the night, came cries of pain—sobbing and wailing, rage and prayer, and screams for help, for God's sake.

Many of the men wore out before dawn and were fordone: hands frozen, feet frozen, lips and throat frozen—heart frozen. And many a man dropped in his tracks, limp and spiritless as rags, and lay still, every man in his own drift of snow; and his soul sped away as though glad to be gone. Brothers, some, and fathers and sons—the one beating the other with frozen hands, and calling to him to rouse and stand up lest he die.

Dawn came. It was just a slow, dirty dusk. And day was no better than dusk. Still they walked blind and tortured in a frosty smother and driving whirlwind of snow. Hands frozen, feet frozen—and the cold creeping in upon the heart! They were numb and worn and sleepy. And there was no rest for them. To pause was to come into living peril—to rest was to sleep; and to sleep was death. Once more, then, when day was full broken, Archie and Billy came on Jonathan Farr and Toby.

The old man was sheathed in snow and frozen

spindrift. A hairy old codger he was—icicles of his own frozen breath clinging to his long white beard and icicles hanging from his bushy brows. And he was beating Toby without mercy: for the lad would fall down, worn out, and whimper and squirm; and the old man would jerk and cuff him to his feet, and drive him on with cuffs from behind, stumbling and whimpering and bawling.

It was a sad task that he had, done in pity—thus to cuff the little lad awake and keep him moving; and Billy Topsail fancied that it was waste pain. It seemed to him that the lad must die in the gale, soon or late—no doubt about that, with stout men yielding to death roundabout. Billy thought that it would be better to let him sleep and die and suffer no more.

"I'm s' sleepy!" Toby complained to his grandfather. "Leave me sleep!"

"Get up!"

"Ah, jus' a minute, gran'pa!"

"Get up!"

"You c'n wake me 's easy ——"

"Get up!"

"Ye hurt me, gran'pa!"

"Drive on!"

"You leave me alone!" Toby bawled, angrily. "Ye hurt!"

"Drive on!"

By this time the men had been more than twenty-four hours on the ice. And they had no food. Hungry? No. They were cold. No man famished in that gale. And they had yet a night of that gale to win through, though they knew nothing about that at the time. They began to stray wide. And they began to go blind. And some men fell in the water and were drowned. Billy Topsail saw John Temple, of Heart's Island, drop through a crust of snow and go down for good and all; and he saw Tom Crutch, of Seldom-Come-By, stumble over the edge of a pan, and heard him screech for help. They hauled him out—two men of his own harbour; and he was frozen solid in half an hour.

Some men chose an end of torture and leaped into the water and killed themselves. And as day drew on, others began to go mad. It was horrible—like a madhouse. They babbled, stark mad—the harbours they came from, and their mothers, their wives, their babies. And they had visions, and were deluded—some saw a blaze of fire and set out to find the glow, and called to the others, as they went off, to come and be warm. And one saw the ship's lights, as in clear, dark weather, and staggered away, bawling that he was coming, with a troop of poor madmen in his wake.

This is the naked truth about that gale.

CHAPTER XL

In Which Toby Farr Falls in the Water, and, Being Soaked to the Skin, Will Freeze Solid in Half an Hour, in the Frosty Dusk of the Approaching Night, Unless a Shift of Dry Clothes is Found, a Necessity Which Sends Jonathan Farr and Billy Topsail Hunting for Dead Men

THROUGH all this black confusion and bitter hardship Billy Topsail and Archie Armstrong wandered with the others of the men of the *Rough and Tumble.* They suffered, despaired, hoped, despaired again—but fought desperately for their lives as partners. When Archie wanted to give way to his overwhelming desire for sleep, Billy cuffed and beat him into wakefulness and renewed courage; and when Billy, worn out and numb with cold, entertained the despair that assaulted him, Archie gathered his faculties and encouraged him. Had either been alone on the floe, it is probable that he would have perished; but both together, devoted to each other, resolved to help each other, each watchful of the other, each inspired by the other's need—fighting thus as partners in peril, they were as well off, in point of vitality and determination, as any man on the floe. Afraid? Yes, they were afraid—that is to say, each perceived the peril he was in, knew that his life hung in the balance, and wished with all his might to live; but neither boy whimpered in a cowardly way.

Coming on dusk of that day, the boys fell in for the last time with old Jonathan Farr. Jonathan had Toby by the scruff of the neck and was just setting him on his feet by a broken crust of snow. Toby was wide awake then. And he was dripping wet to the waist—near to the armpits. And he was frightened.

"I falled in," said he. "I—I stumbled."

In that wind and frost it was death. The lad was doomed. And it was but a matter of minutes.

"Is you—is you wet through, Toby?" Jonathan asked, blankly.

"I is, sir."

Jonathan drew off a mitt and felt of the lad's clothes from his calves to his waist.

"Wet through!" said he. "Oh, dear me!"

"I'm soppin' t' the skin."

"Jus' drippin' wet!"

"I'm near froze," Toby complained. And he chilled. And his teeth clicked. "I wisht I had a shift o' clothes," said he.

"I wisht you had!" said Jonathan.

Billy Topsail got to windward of Jonathan to speak his mind in the old man's ear. It seemed to Billy that Toby's case was hopeless. The lad would freeze. There was no help for it. And the sooner his suffering was over—the better.

"Let un die," Billy pleaded.

Jonathan shook his head and flashed at Billy. Yet Billy had spoken kindness and plain wisdom. But Jonathan was in a rage with him. Billy heard his icicles rattle. And Jonathan glared in wrath through the white fringe of his brows.

"Go to!" he exclaimed.

"My pants is froze stiff!" said Toby in amazement. "That's comical! I can't move me legs." And then he whimpered with pain and misery and fear. "I'll freeze stiff!" said he. "I'll die!"

It was coming fast.

"You can't save un," Billy insisted, in Jonathan's ear. "He'll freeze afore dark. Let un go."

"I'll never give up," Jonathan protested.

"I'm awful mis'able, gran'pa," said Toby. "What'll I do now?"

"Ah, have mercy!" Billy begged. "Let un slip away quick an' be gone."

Jonathan peered around.

"Mus' be some dead men, Billy," said he, "lyin' around here somewheres."

Dead men enough in the drifts!

"More than a hundred," said Archie. "I counted a hundred and nine through the day."

"I'll find one," said Jonathan.

"No time, Jonathan."

"They're lyin' handy. I fell over Jack Brace somewheres near here."

"Night's closin'," said Billy.

"No time t' lose," Jonathan agreed.

"Speed then!" Billy exclaimed. "He'll freeze fast afore you find one."

"Guard the lad," said Jonathan. "I'll not be long. Try his temper. He'll fight if you tease un."

With that, then, old Jonathan Farr ran off to dig a dead man from the drifts. The boys could not see him in the snow. All this while the wind was biting and pushing and choking them still

—the snow was mixed with the first dusk. Toby was shivering then—cowering from the wind, head down. And he was dull. His head nodded. He swayed in the wind—caught his feet; and he jerked himself awake—and nodded and swayed again. Billy Topsail thought it a pity and a wrong to rouse him. Yet both boys turned to to keep him warm.

Toby must have the life kept in him, they thought, until his grandfather got back. And they cuffed him and teased him until his temper was hot, poor lad, and he fought them in a passion—stumbling at them, hampered by his frozen clothes, and striking at them with his stiff arms and icy fists.

Jonathan came then.

"I can't find no dead men," he panted. It was hard for him to breast the wind. He was gasping with haste and fear. "I've hunted," said he, "an' I can't find no dead men."

"They're lyin' thick hereabouts," said Billy.

"They're all covered up. I can't find un."

"Did you kick the drifts?" Archie asked.

"We've strayed wide," said Jonathan. "I can't find no dead men. An' I can't walk well no more."

"Watch the lad," said Billy. "I'll try my hand."

Toby was lying down. Jonathan caught him up from the ice and held him in his arms.

"Quick!" he cried. "He've fell asleep. Ah, he's freezin'!"

It was coming dark fast. There was no time to waste in the gale that was blowing. The frost was putting Toby to sleep. Billy sped. He searched the drifts like a dog for a dead man. And soon he had luck. He found Long Jerry Cuff, of Providence Arm, a chunk of ice, poor man!—lying in a cuddle, arms folded and knees drawn up, like a child snuggled in bed. Long Jerry had been in the water, soaked to the skin, and he was solid and useless. And then Billy came on a face and a fur cap in a drift of snow. It was George Hunt, of Bullet Bight, with whom Billy had once sailed, in fishing weather, to Thumb-and-Finger of the Labrador.

Long Jerry was lying flat on his back with his arms flung out and his legs spread. And he was frozen fast to the floe. Billy could not budge him. No. Billy caught him by the head and lifted—he was stiff as a plank; and Billy failed. And Billy took him by the foot and pried a leg loose—and ripped at it with all his might; and again he failed. Solid as stone! They must all have been solid like that. And then Billy knew that it was no use to try any more—that they could not strip the clothes from a dead man if they had a dead man to strip.

And then he went disconsolate to Jonathan.

CHAPTER XLI

In Which a Dead Man is Made to Order for Little Toby Farr

"COULDN'T you find none?" cried Jonathan.

"Yes."

"Where is he?"

"No use, Jonathan. He's froze fast t' the ice. I couldn't budge un."

"We'll all ——"

Billy shook his head.

"No use, Jonathan," he said again. "He's hard as stone. We couldn't strip un."

Jonathan said nothing to that. He was in a muse. Presently he looked up.

Then he said:

"It don't matter."

"How's Toby?" Billy asked.

Toby was on his feet.

"I'm all right," he answered for himself. "Isn't I doin' pretty well for me, gran'pa?"

"You is!"

Billy took Jonathan aside. Jonathan was at ease. Billy marvelled. It was queer.

"I've warmed un up again," said Jonathan. "Archie an' me done well. We've got un quite warm."

"Too bad," said Billy. "He've got t' die."

"No," said Jonathan. "I've a shot in the locker, Billy. I've found a way. Heed me, Billy. An' mark well what I says. I 'low a dead man's clothes would be cold an' damp anyhow. The lad needs a shift o' warm clothes. An' I'm warm, Billy. An' my underclothes is dry. I been warm an' dry all day long, an' wonderful strong an' wakeful, too, with the fear o' losin' Toby. I'll jus' go away a little piece an' lie down an' die. I'm tired an' dull. It won't take long. An' you an' Archie will strip me, Billy, while I'm still warm."

"It might do."

"'Tis the only sensible thing t' do."

It was the only thing to do. Billy Topsail knew that. If Toby Farr's life were to be saved, he must have dry clothes at once. Billy did not offer to strip himself for Toby. It would have been mock heroics. Nor did Archie Armstrong when he learned of what Jonathan was to do.

Either boy would have risked his life in a moment to save the life of Toby Farr—without a second thought, an instant of hesitation, whatever the risk. Obviously it was the duty of old Jonathan Farr to make the only sacrifice that could save the boy. Had Archie or Billy volunteered, the old man would have thanked them and declined the gift.

As old Jonathan had said, to die was the only sensible thing to do.

"Nothin' else t' do," said Billy.

"No; nothin' else t' do that I can think of right now."

"'Tis hard for you, Jonathan," said Billy.

"Oh, no!" Jonathan replied. "I don't mind."

"Then make haste," Billy advised. "If 'tis t' be done, it must be done quick."

"Don't waste no heat," said Jonathan. "Fetch Toby alongside, jus' as soon as I'm gone, an' strip me afore I'm cold."

"Ay," Billy agreed. "That's a good idea."

"An' you keep Toby alive, somehow, Billy," Jonathan went on. "God help you!"

"I will."

Jonathan moved away.

"Watch where I goes," said he. "Don't lose me. I won't be far."

And then Toby, whom Archie had in hand, keeping him moving, spoke in alarm:

"Where you goin', gran'pa?" he demanded.

Jonathan stopped dead. He turned. And he made back towards Toby. And then he stopped dead again.

"I'm jus' goin' t' look for something," said he.

"What you goin' t' look for?"

"I'm goin' t' find a shift o' warm clothes for you."

"A dead man, gran'pa?"

"Ay; a dead man."

"Don't be long," said Toby. "I'll miss you."

"I'm glad o' that," Jonathan replied.

"You might get lost in the snow," said Toby. "Hurry up. I'll wait here with Billy an' Archie."

"I'll be back jus' as quick as I'm able," Jonathan promised. "You wait here, Toby, an' mind Billy and Archie, won't you, while I'm gone?"

"Ay, sir. An' I'll keep movin' jus' the same as if you was here. Hurry up."

By and by, when Billy thought it was time, he went to where Jonathan was lying.

"Is you dead?" he whispered.

"Not yet," said Jonathan. "Come back in a few minutes."

Pretty soon Billy went back.

"Is you dead?" he asked.

"Not yet," said Jonathan. "I'm makin' poor work of it."

And Billy went once more.

"Is you dead?"

"I'm goin' fast."

And yet again:

"Is you dead?"

And Jonathan was dead.

It was worth doing. It saved Toby Farr alive from that gale. It was no easy thing to clothe him anew in the wind—the little boy weeping for his dead grandfather and wanting to lie down and die by his side. Newfoundland born, however, and used to weather, he lived through the night. And when Cap'n Saul gathered the dead from the ice in the quiet weather of the next morning, the lad was carried aboard and stowed away, frost-bitten in a sad way, yet bound to hang on to life.

Toby said never a word about his grandfather

then. Nor did he weep any more. Nor did he ask Billy and Archie any questions. But he brooded. And the boys wondered what he was thinking so deeply about. And then they put into port—flag at half-mast and a hundred and twenty-one men piled forward like cord-wood. And Toby Farr came on deck, clad in his grandfather's clothes, and watched the dead go ashore, with Archie and Billy and Sir Archibald, until his grandfather went by, wrapped in a Union Jack.

"Billy!" said he.

"Ay, Toby?"

"Did my gran'pa gimme his clothes?"

"He did."

"I'll be worthy!" said Toby.

And he has grown up since then. And he is worthy.

CHAPTER XLII

In Which the Tale Comes to a Good End: Archie and Billy Make Ready for Dinner, Toby Farr is Taken for Good and All by Sir Archibald, and Billy Topsail, Having Been Declared Wrong by Archie's Father, Takes the Path That Leads to a New Shingle, After Which the Author Asks a Small Favour of the Reader

WELL, now, we have come to the end of the tale of Billy Topsail. I need not describe the grief of the Colony when the tragedy of the ice-floes was disclosed. Newfoundlanders are warm-hearted folk; they are easily touched to sympathy—they grieved, indeed, even to the remotest harbours, when news of the death of the men of the *Rough and Tumble* was spread forth. It was a catastrophe that impended every sealing season—rare, perhaps, in its degree, but forever a thing to be expected. Yet you are not to think of Newfoundland in visions wholly of wind and snow and ice. Newfoundland is not an Arctic country by any means. Nor does the wind blow all the while; nor is the sea all the while in a turmoil. It is a lovely coast after all; and the folk who live there are simple, self-respecting, cheerful—a lovable, admirable folk. To be sure they have summer weather. What is written in this book is of the spring of the year—the tempestuous season, with the ice breaking up. As a matter of fact, Newfoundland seems to me, in retrospect, to be far less a land of tempest and frost than of sunlit hills and a rippling blue sea.

Ashore, at last, and making ready for dinner, in Sir Archibald Armstrong's great house, while Archie's mother mothered little Toby Farr, who was to live in the great house thereafter, and be reared by Sir Archibald, like a brother of Archie's own—alone in Archie's rooms, Billy and Archie talked a little while.

"Somehow, Archie," said Billy, with a puzzled frown, "it didn't seem nothin' much t' do at the time."

"What, Billy?"

"What Jonathan done."

"No," Archie agreed.

"Somehow," Billy went on, "it jus' seemed as if everybody was dyin', or goin' t' die, an' one more wouldn't make no very great difference. Didn't it seem that way t' you, Archie?"

"Just that way, Billy."

"Queer, isn't it?"

"I didn't care very much, Billy, what happened to me."

"Nor I what happened t' me."

"Sometimes I *wanted* to die. I just wanted to lie down and ——"

"Me too, Archie."

"Looking back, though, it isn't the same. I'm glad I'm alive."

There was a silence.

"Archie," said Billy, "that was a pretty fine thing that Jonathan done."

"It was, Billy."

"An' the way he done it was fine. It was a man's way t' do a thing like that. No fuss about it. Jus' a quiet way—jus' goin' ahead an' doin' what he thought he ought t' do, an' sayin' nothin' about it."

"That was the best of it, Billy."

"It was a *great* thing, Archie. I can't get over it. I thinks of it again an' again an' again. I'd like t' be big enough t' do a thing like that in jus' that way."

"And I, Billy."

"I bet you, Archie, Jonathan was *glad* t' be able t' do it."

"I think he was."

"Yes," Billy repeated; "a big thing like that in a big way like that. I'd like t' be man enough. An' I knows only one other man in the world who could do it—in jus' that quiet way."

"Who's that, Billy?"

"Doctor Luke."

"Yes," Archie agreed; "he's big enough for anything."

"I'd like t' be like he!" Billy sighed.

Then the boys went down to dinner. Archie had something in mind of which Billy Topsail was not aware.

After dinner, Toby Farr was put to bed. He was a soft little fellow, perhaps, and Archie's mother, too, was tender. At any rate, she was calling Toby "Son" by that time; and Toby didn't mind, and Archie was delighted, and Sir Archibald was smiling as though he enjoyed it. Toby was not happy—not by any means; no prospect of luxury, no new love, could ease the wish for his grandfather's voice and presence. Yet he was as happy as he very well could be—and as safe as any lad ever was. When he said good-night, he said it gravely, in the mannerly way he had—a courteous voice, a serious air, a little bow. Sir Archibald smiled, and Archie clapped him on the back, and Archie's mother put her arms around the lad, smiling, too, and led him off to stow him away.

Archie and Billy were then left alone with Sir Archibald.

"Dad," Archie began, "Billy and I have been talking."

"Well, well!" said Sir Archibald.

Billy chuckled.

"I mean *really* talking, dad."

"What about, son?"

"Well, quite a number of things."

"You surprise me!" said Sir Archibald.

Archie ignored the banter.

"Look here, dad," he said, "I want Billy to do something that he won't do."

"Then," said Sir Archibald, "I should recommend you to ask him to do something else."

"But that won't do."

"Must he do this thing?"

"If it's right."

"Is it right?"

"*I* think so."

"What is it?"

Archie explained the matter in dispute, with all its provisions for guarding Billy Topsail's self-respect, and Sir Archibald listened.

"I agree with you," said Sir Archibald, promptly, when Archie came to the end. "I think it right."

And that is how Billy Topsail found a proper way to study medicine—that is how it came about that a new shingle declares to the world of the north Newfoundland Coast the whereabouts of—

WILLIAM TOPSAIL, M. D.

You may find Billy Topsail in the surgery (when he happens to be at home) if you land from the mail-boat and follow the road over Tinkle-Tinkle Hill to Broad Cove—a hearty, smiling, rather quiet chap, of a scientific turn, who goes where he is called, and has the reputation of being the most promising physician and surgeon in Newfoundland. He has been advised to go to St. John's, of course; but that he will not do—for reasons of his own, which have to do with the obligations of service. Well, then, there he is—in the surgery, when he is at home; and if you *should* happen to go ashore from the mail-boat, and if you should take Tinkle-Tinkle Road to Broad Cove, and if your seeking eye should alight upon a new shingle, inscribed WILLIAM TOPSAIL, M. D., and if you should knock on the door, and if a stalwart, fine-looking, rather quiet chap, with a twinkling smile, should open the door, and if you should tell him that you know me, and that I had invited you to call —

He'll laugh. And he'll say:

"Come in! Glad t' see you!"

And you go in—don't fail to. You'll have a good time. And give Billy my compliments and tell him I'll be up to see him one of these summers. Thanks. I'm much obliged.

Printed in the United States of America

CPSIA information can be obtained at www.ICGtesting.com
Printed in the USA
267998BV00002B/71-74/P

9 781177 132022